2020

VISIONS FOR THE CENTRAL VALLEY

Edited by Amy Moffat

Heyday Books, Berkeley, California
Great Valley Center, Modesto, California

This project was generously funded in part by The California Endowment.

The publisher thanks the James Irvine Foundation for their support of Central Valley publishing.

The Great Valley Center would like to thank the contributors for generously allowing their speeches to be transcribed, edited, and reprinted.

Library of Congress Cataloging-in-Publication Data
2020 : visions for the Central Valley / edited by Amy Moffat.
    p. cm.
 Keynote speeches from the conference held by the the Great Valley Center in May 2009.
 Includes bibliographical references.
 ISBN 978-1-59714-133-8 (pbk. : alk. paper)
 1. Central Valley (Calif.)--Economic conditions--21st century. 2. Central Valley (Calif.)--Social conditions--21st century. 3. Central Valley (Calif. : Valley)--Economic conditions--21st century. 4. Central Valley (Calif. : Valley)--Social conditions--21st century. I. Moffat, Amy. II. Great Valley Center. III. Title: Visions for the Central Valley.
 HC107.C22C4155 2010
 307.109794'5--dc22

Cover Art: Shutterstock
Cover Design: The Book Designers
Interior Design/Typesetting: Rebecca LeGates
Printing and Binding: Thomson-Shore, Dexter, MI

Orders, inquiries, and correspondence should be addressed to:
    Heyday Books
    P. O. Box 9145, Berkeley, CA 94709
    (510) 549-3564, Fax (510) 549-1889
    www.heydaybooks.com

10 9 8 7 6 5 4 3 2 1

CONTENTS

Introduction
Amy Moffat

California's Great Central Valley is changing. The region, which consists of nineteen counties and stretches over four hundred and fifty miles, from Redding to Bakersfield, is rapidly growing. From 1995 to 2005, the Valley gained more than one million residents. A decade from now, the Valley's population is expected to be 8.7 million, a 52 percent increase from 2000. Though agriculture is giving way to urban uses, the Valley still accounts for more than $23 billion in agricultural revenue—more than any state in the nation. Wealth for some is building while poverty for many worsens. Traffic delays are increasing and so is pollution. Asthma and obesity are on the rise. Neighborhoods are becoming more diverse as housing, energy, jobs, education, and health needs shift.

In preparation for this growth, today's leaders and residents are at a critical junction in balancing economic, social, and environmental priorities. Whose idea of the future will come to pass? Who stands to gain and what will be lost? What is the path to a better future in the Valley, and what are the resources needed to travel it successfully? Do we want to continue to be among the poorest regions in the nation and in danger of having a substandard workforce, short of water, and long on chronic medical problems? The stakes are enormously high and in the coming years many people will advocate for competing interests and different visions.

In May 2009, the Great Valley Center convened its annual conference in Sacramento, themed "20/20 Foresight: A View of the Great Valley in a Decade." A dynamic gathering of people listened and interacted with thought leaders and experts who attempted to address these and other timely questions about health, community well-being, agriculture, transportation, land use, energy, water, and natural resources. The idea was to look ahead to the future rather than dwell on the past. As David Hosley, the Great Valley Center's president, put it, "A look ahead to the year 2020 will help chart the path to a better future and provide information about trends and positive steps that might be taken in the next decade." The conference provided vital insights into the current social, economic, and environmental conditions in California's Great Central Valley, and though speakers urgently warned of the consequences of maintaining the status quo, they also gave hope for a prosperous future.

This book features edited transcriptions of five keynote speeches given at the conference. In "The Sustainability Imperative," L. Hunter Lovins, president and founder of Natural Capitalism Solutions, shares insights on how businesses can invest in energy efficiency and get their biggest return on investments. Quentin Kopp, chair of the California High Speed Rail Authority, describes the plan for high-speed rail service to be built through the Central Valley to connect Los Angeles and the San Francisco Bay Area in his speech "Designing the Transportation of the Future." "A Thriving Agriculture in the Twenty-First Century" presents insights by A. G. Kawamura, secretary of California's Department of Food and Agriculture, about the current conditions of California agriculture and the importance of putting together an agricultural plan for the state. In "The Delta's Age of Reason, " Jeff Mount, director of the Center for Watershed Sciences at UC Davis, uses humor and hard science to explain controversial water issues in the Sacramento–San Joaquin Delta. Last, Richard Pan, a pediatrician at UC Davis and founder of Communities and Physicians Together, explores how many different types of environments, physical and social, affect key health disparities in "A Community Approach to Health and Health Care." At the end of each chapter a "Valley-Wise Living" section provides key actions that you, as an individual, can take between now and 2020 for a sustainable Valley; a "Resources" section lists different books and reports to read on the subject, as well as websites to browse; and a "Food for Thought" section offers questions that you can bring to your organization, agency, or business to facilitate discussion and strategic planning. These compilations provide you the opportunity to apply this information to your own work, now, to see results in a decade—a time frame within which most of you will still be able to be active participants.

While the individual chapters may seem isolated in the focus of their topics, many threads tie the topics together. One key theme is choice and the privilege of having choices, whether they consist of what foods to buy or how we address difficult issues, like water management. Another common focus is on the predictability of the region's problems; the past might be a predictor of the future, but we can make changes so that the future is not dictated by the past. These speakers frequently dispel common myths that affect the general public's ideas about certain issues: both Kawamura and Mount are concerned that the public has inaccurate information about how much water is used by agriculture and other sectors, for example, and Lovins points out that the common idea that it is bad to turn computers off and on not only is an urban myth but has serious energy consequences. Several speakers caution against allowing general opinion, rather than empirical evidence or evidence-based research, to drive policy. Not all the speakers agree with each other. Some of the statements across the chapters contradict and conflict. The purpose is not to define the answers, but to provide information so you can make your own informed choices.

Though the speakers often point out discouraging trends and serious challenges that the region and its residents face, each is also deeply optimistic about our capacity to address these issues in creative and innovative ways. Without the active participation of informed policy makers and residents alike, a bleak future seems set in stone. But the Valley is as rich in social resources—people, ideas, traditions, and cultures—as it is in natural ones, and, as Richard Pan points out, "it is also going to be about people coming together in their communities, saying this is what we want for our community, and then working together to move that forward." L. Hunter Lovins powerfully sums it up: "The future of this Great Valley is in your hands. It is not fate. There are drivers of change that are coming at you… How you respond to them will determine whether or not your children are going to want to live in this Valley."

The Sustainability Imperative

L. Hunter Lovins

It may seem to outsiders that the Central Valley is obsessed with the concept of sustainability. But we live in a fast-growing area where problems will only be exacerbated by going forward with the status quo. The next decade will be critical to balance the economic, social, and environmental priorities to plan and achieve long-term community well-being.

The Central Valley of California is at a critical juncture in energy consumption. The Valley is growing 50 percent faster than the rest of California, yet the cost of energy is outpacing that growth. We are seeing significant changes in the Sierra snowpack and that is affecting hydroelectricity, and a great deal of electricity in the Valley is used just to move water. Unless we can significantly change the way people in the region do business and conduct their personal lives, at-risk families and even moderate-income people will be unable to have the quality of life we experience today. By nearly every indicator, the economic health of Valley residents lags behind that of our state and nation. More than a third of the population does not speak English as their first language. Few of those living in poverty are focused on renewable energy. But they represent, along with rural residents, an important opportunity to reduce energy consumption.

In the Central Valley, the huge growth coming in the decades ahead requires new approaches to energy conservation, and a much higher commitment on the part of organizations and individuals to live differently. Incremental improvement will not suffice when it comes to renewable resources. In this chapter L. Hunter Lovins asserts that it is imperative that everyone start living and operating their businesses in more sustainable ways, the good news being that sustainable measures are surprisingly cost-effective and make good business sense.

L. Hunter Lovins is president and founder of Natural Capitalism Solutions in Colorado. Natural Capitalism Solutions works to educate senior decision makers in business, government, and civil society to restore and enhance natural and human capital while increasing prosperity and quality of life. Trained as a sociologist and lawyer, Ms. Lovins also cofounded the California Conservation Project and Rocky Mountain Institute, and has consulted for scores of industries and governments worldwide. Lovins's areas of expertise include natural capitalism, sustainable development, globalization, energy and resource policy, economic development, climate change, land management, and fire rescue and emergency medicine.

Lovins received her Juris Doctorate from Loyola University School of Law, has taught at dozens of universities, including an engagement as the Henry R. Luce Visiting Professor at Dartmouth College, and is currently a founding professor of business at the Presidio School of Management, one of the first accredited programs offering an MBA in sustainable management. She has coauthored nine books and dozens of papers and articles, some of which have recently appeared in *World Link, World Business Academy Review, American Prospect,* and the *Los Angeles Times.* She has been the recipient of several honors, including *Time* magazine's Hero of the Planet in 2000.

The Sustainability Imperative

You have an opportunity with the future of the Great Valley. The Great Valley has been the breadbasket of America, and it could be the breadbasket of the world if you decide not to pave it over. These are not questions of fate, they are questions of choice.

The economic woes are well known. The Chinese curse: May you live in interesting times.

California is one of the leading states now in the country for unemployment, fourth highest.[1] Housing prices are collapsing, and what are we going to do about a state budget? The *Wall Street Journal* wrote not too long ago about the "end of excess," pointing out that we've been losing, in the nation, over six hundred thousand jobs a month for the last two or three months. Fifty trillion dollars gone! Where did it go? I asked this question the other night and a woman said, "Money heaven." That may not be a bad answer. Consumer spending contract-

> **"These are not questions of fate, they are questions of choice."**

ing, construction spending contracting. The International Monetary Fund recently said that thirty of the thirty-four advanced economies are expected to shrink in the greatest collapse since World War II, and the U.S. continues shrinking through 2010.

It was Edward Abbey who said it best: "Growth for the sake of growth is the ideology of the cancer cell." It is sunk into our minds, particularly if we are local businesspeople, or local government people, that we have to grow. Grow or we die. And yet that is not true of any healthful organism on

3

the planet. So this debate about growth needs to come up and be a topic of polite conversation. In many communities if you raise this question, you will be shot, run out of town on a rail, stoned, or perhaps worse, laughed at. And I expect many of you know what I am saying. So let us reframe the debate. What is it that we want more of? Growth. Well, what does growth mean? What do we want to have grow? Some people say the GNP. What is the GNP? A divorcing cancer patient that gets in a car wreck has added to the GNP, but is she any better off? Clearly not. So in our communities, let us start a conversation about what we want more of: fun, health, time with our families, education, learning, culture, music, art. There are a lot of things that we can have more of, that do not run down the natural or human capital of the planet. We can also enlarge this conversation by asking, "What are the constituent elements of wealth?"

> "...what we want more of: fun, health, time with our families, education, learning, culture, music, art. There are a lot of things that we can have more of, that do not run down the natural or human capital of the planet."

We are facing some fairly formidable **drivers of change**. This is a term Royal Dutch Shell uses when it does scenario planning, when it tries to understand plausible stories about how the future could evolve. When you find a driver of change you know that business as usual will not endure. We are facing some formidable ones. We are losing every major ecosystem on the planet. We live in a carbon constrained world, if not a global climate crisis. We have economic instability, volatile energy prices (they are now back above fifty dollars a barrel and headed north). Every bit of our infrastructure is vulnerable. China and India, "Chindia," are in the world market for eventually everything. Remember a year ago today, gas prices were over five dollars a gallon and China and India buying, essentially, every commodity? Water. This is your lifeblood but it is the lifeblood of the entire planet and it is in short supply. Food. We have had food riots on three continents. And then what I call the **sustainability imperative**. Collectively, these are going to change everything about your life, your business, and life in this Great Valley.

Lester Brown[2] points out that if China continues to grow at a rate that it is believed it must to avoid revolution, by 2030 it will need ninety-nine million barrels of oil a day—that is more oil than the world now lifts or probably can ever lift—and more cars and cotton and concrete. And at that point the future is not possible. When you realize the future is not possible, you are staring at a driver of change. We are going to change the way we do business.

Climate change. It is very much for real. My particular concern is for the rivers that come out of the Himalaya that water about two-thirds of the people on Earth. The glaciers in the Himalaya are already retreating. If you want to see the face of climate change, look at Australia, where the Murray-Darling Basin used to run bank to bank but now runs dry and can no longer support the growing of rice. So farmers in Australia are starting to commit suicide.

You have water constraints here. Farming is a good use of the state's water and climate models show that the availability of water is going to be dropping: a 20 percent reduction in runoff by 2050 means nearly nine out of every ten water deliveries will be missed. Steven Chu[3] says that agriculture in California may cease to exist and he is not quite sure how the cities will survive. We almost saw that this year, but thank God for the rains. But the rains under the climate modeling are going to be less predictable. Jim Hansen,[4] the great NASA scientist, said, "Don't ask what's possible, ask what's necessary."

What is necessary is 350. This is 350 parts per million concentration of carbon in the atmosphere. This is the level the scientists are now saying may be what they call "safe level." That means there is a fifty-fifty chance we will not have a catastrophe. That is not what you or I would consider safe. We are now at 387, which means we are going to have to cut back on the amount of carbon that is already in the atmosphere. Scientists like Holmes Hummel[5] say, "No more carbon emissions." And Dr. Hansen says that if the U.S. fails to act in the next year it may become impractical to prevent "disastrous climate changes that spiral dynamically out of humanity's control." This is sobering.

We need a miracle. If you look at the weight and magnitude issue, how fast it takes to turn over a stock—ask our utility friends how fast big infrastructures turn over—it is about fifty years. We do not have fifty years. That means we are going to get very creative.

Bill Becker[6] said, "If we insist on ruining the planet, we're going to have to stop claiming we're a superior species." And Ray Anderson[7] asked, "What's the business case for ending life on Earth?"

The science is uncertain. We do not know how bad it is going to be; we do not know how fast it is coming at us. Scientists are scrambling to get the models to match up with observed reality. The science does not matter, and I say this with all deference to the scientists who are working very hard on these issues. But let us assume the skeptics are right. Frankly, do not go to Vegas on those odds, but if all you care about is being a profit-maximizing capitalist, you will do exactly the same thing you would do if you were scared to death of climate change, because we know how to solve this problem at a profit. The smart companies are starting to do it.

Ten years ago or more, DuPont announced they were going to cut their emissions of greenhouse gases 65 percent below their 1990 levels by 2010. This is somewhat more ambitious than what our past federal administration said we could not possibly do—that it would bankrupt the economy to try to cut American emissions 7 percent below 1990 levels. Has DuPont joined Greenpeace? They made this announcement in the name of increasing shareholder value, and they have done rather well. They are already down 80 percent below their 1990 levels for a savings (from 2000 to 2005) of three billion dollars. Andrew Winston,[8] author of the book *Green to Gold,* points out that DuPont's efforts to squeeze out waste are adding up to $2.2 billion a year. Guess what their profitability is: $2.2 billion a year. This is a company that is profitable because it is squeezing out waste.

STMicroelectronics committed to zero net CO_2 emissions by 2010, carbon neutral, with a forty-fold increase in production over 1990 by 2010. When Pasquale Pistorio[9] made this announcement, he had no earthly idea how to do it. Figuring it out is driving their corporate innovation, taking ST from being the number-twelve chip maker in the world to number six. They are winning awards (2004 Best Industrial Renewable Energy Partnership from the EU). They recognize that by the time they become climate neutral, they will have saved about $900 million.

The insurance industry is getting involved. The European reinsurers—they insure the insurance industry—are starting to say, "If your company does not take its carbon footprint seriously, maybe our company does not want to insure you, or your officers and directors." Imagine doing business without D&O insurance.

The banks are starting to issue an index of bond issuances based on companies' carbon footprints. The Carbon Disclosure Project out of the United Kingdom six or eight years ago sent out to the Financial Times 500—the five hundred biggest companies on earth—a little survey asking, "What's your carbon footprint?" For a few years everybody ignored it, until about three years ago, when 60 percent of the biggest companies on Earth answered. Last year, over 77 percent of the now FT 1,800 companies answered. Why? For one thing the Carbon Disclosure Project represents institutional investors with over $50 trillion in assets. If you are going to go to the capital marketplace, we might want to answer their questions. And for another, under the Sarbanes-Oxley Act of 2002—the new U.S. corporate ethics law that emerged from the Enron and Worldcom scandals—if as a manager you to fail to disclose to the shareholders information that can materially affect the value of stock, you can be personally criminally liable. So, what is your carbon footprint?

We walked into a company that had sixty-three hundred computers and printers they left on twenty-four hours a day, seven days a week. They had urban myths that if you turn them off and then turn them on, it shortens the lifetime of the computers. No, not true. IT has to have them left on all the time. No, not true. Turning them off except for one night a week would save the company $700,000 in the first year. In this country, we waste $2.8 billion a year leaving computers on when we are not using them. And this is about a quarter of the cost of energy in a modern office building.

We walked into another company, a distribution center (I know you have a few of those in the Central Valley). This was a seven-million-square-foot center that had five-hundred-watt lightbulbs shining down on the tops of boxes, because that is what a distribution center is—it is floor-to-ceiling boxes. The guys down below had task lighting so they could see where they were going. We said, "Y'all have a switch?" $650,000 was saved in the first year.

At UC Davis you have the California Lighting Technology Center,[10] which can help any of you—whether you are a homeowner, a business, a government—replace lights with LED lights with more efficient lighting schemes. And they have got the science behind it and they have got the numbers behind it. Check it out.

I consult for very big businesses, but the businesses in your towns are the lifeblood of our economy. Small business is roughly half the economy, 90 percent of the nongovernmental employers, and nobody is really working with them. At Natural Capital Solutions we are in the process of bringing out a manual for small businesses, a web-based learning tool called "Solutions at the Speed of Business"[11] that would be like having a personal tutor moving at your pace, enabling you to cut carbon emissions profitably. Commercial buildings use 18 percent of the total energy in the U.S. Just take lighting: changing out incandescent lightbulbs to compact fluorescents—never mind going all the way to LEDs—will save you about 75 percent of your lighting energy. There is a whole array of measures, which are also included in the Great Valley Center's Energy Primer. Take advantage of this. These are dollars that are leaving your community.

For example, a Re/Max real estate office down in Ft. Lauderdale was doing a remodel, so while they were at it they put in energy saving measures and mostly used a caulk gun. I mean, this is not rocket science here, folks. All exterior windows and doors were sealed and caulked and the ductwork was resealed. They saved $7,900 the first year, largely from eliminating unnecessary air-conditioning.

> "Investing in energy efficiency is your biggest return on investment."

The return on investment (ROI) of climate protection measures is enormous. Fluorescent lamps and fixtures: 40 percent return on investment. You tell me where your 401(k) is going to get that kind of an ROI. Investing in energy efficiency is your biggest return on investment. Where? Buildings. Most of us spend 90 percent of our time in buildings and they are responsible for a lot of energy use, a lot of electricity use—about 70 percent in the country, and 30 to 60 percent of greenhouse gas emissions, depending on where you are, and a lot of other waste. We can take any existing building and make it three- or four-fold more efficient, new ones ten times as efficient, and they work better. PG&E has shown that if you put features like daylighting into schools, you will get 20 to 26 percent higher test scores. Wal-Mart found that by putting daylighting into Wal-Marts, they get higher retail sales by 40 percent. And you will also get higher labor productivity—6 to 16 percent increased labor productivity—and you get decreased worker absenteeism from sick time. Improving indoor air quality could save U.S. businesses $58 billion in avoided sick time each year, and another $200 billion earned in increased worker performance.[12] What you pay for people is about one hundred times what you pay for energy, but how you manage your energy is what enables you to get that productivity boost from people.

The environmental radicals at McKinsey, the big consulting firm, did a little study in which they put all of the measures to cut carbon, all the energy saving measures, various supply measures on the same piece of paper, and surprise! The energy saving measures will about pay for the supply measures, which is to say that we can begin to de-carbonize the economy at no cost if we are smart about it, if we use these saving measures to pay for the new supply.

Now if I have not convinced you that there is an opportunity here, let us start to look at some of the threats.

If you really want to give yourself nightmares, go read the book *Twilight in the Desert* by Matthew Simmons, a Houston oil banker.[13] He points out that the extraction history of the super giant oil fields looks very like a theory put forth by a man named M. King Hubbert in the 1950s.[14] Hubbert was a Shell geologist who said that if you have a finite resource—and it is a corollary of the round earth theory that oil is finite—and you have exponentially growing demand, 90 percent of the oil ever used by people has been since 1958, half of it since 1984; you fall off the production curve as steeply as you went up when you are halfway through the resource, not when you have exhausted the resource. Hubbard said the U.S. would hit peak oil around 1970; it appears we did. He said the world would hit its peak about now; we may be hitting it. Remember those Chinese and Indians behind them wanting more oil than the world now lifts? If your economy, if your life, if your business, if your community depends on petroleum…think about this. Last year when the oil prices were at $150 per barrel, this country was borrowing $2 billion a day, largely from the Chinese, to buy imported oil. We are running out. We are running out of time, and we are running out of oil. If we use oil at our current global consumption rate, we will run out in thirty-three years. If the U.S. uses only oil left in U.S. fields, that is three years' worth. If the U.S. uses all of Iraq's oil, it will run out in fifteen years. If the whole world consumes at the U.S. rate, that is six years.

There are answers. We used to be able to go from Boston to St. Louis never leaving a trolley car. In Europe, people commute by bicycle. How about high-speed trains? If you still want to drive a car, we know how to make cars that get one hundred miles to the gallon. This is not a red or a blue issue.

Jim Woolsey,[15] who used to run the CIA, has a plug-in electric hybrid run off solar panels on his roof with a bumper sticker on the back: "Osama bin Laden hates my car." He says this is a national security issue. And he said, "Look, we're fighting both sides of the war on terror. We pay for our guys and we buy oil from the guys who pay for the bad guys." This is silly. We can get fuel from different sources.

I was on the podium with Richard Branson[16] and Bill Clinton when Branson said he is putting the profits of the Virgin Group for the next ten years into carbon neutral fuel. The media came running up and asked why. He said, "I run an airline. We live in a carbon-restrained world. I'm going to need fuel." So Virgin has already flown a jet from Heathrow, in London, to Amsterdam Airport Schiphol on a quarter biodiesel. Air New Zealand has flown a jet on half biodiesel and half jet fuel.

It typically takes more energy and water to grow a bushel of corn than the energy content of the corn. The average molecule of food travels twenty-five hundred miles before somebody eats it, and tastes like it. And there is a growing movement, particularly in Europe, but also in this country, for things like the 100 mile diet, slow food—this is food that you actually enjoy, coming together and cooking and eating in a civilized fashion. People are starting to grow their own gardens again.

The Germans think peak oil will hit next year. The International Energy Agency said to expect serious constraints on the supply of oil within the next year to two years. If peak oil hits, everything about the way we do agriculture is going to change in a hurry. Where will your food come from? Now, in California you are in a much better place than, say, the East Coast, which will starve within three days if you drop three bridges across the Mississippi, because they do not grow their own food. But how many of you in this Great Valley grow food that you can actually eat?

"We can and need to begin thinking of soil as one of our most valuable resources. It is not dirt."

It is really important, though, that we source the feedstock sustainably. Much of the way we do agriculture now is unsustainable. It is dependent itself on massive energy inputs, on hazardous materials. Corn ethanol subsidized using 150-year-old distillation technology to pour the resulting fuel into inefficient cars is just not smart. We can and need to begin thinking of soil as one of our most valuable resources. It is not dirt. It is, among other things, a way of soaking carbon out of the air and putting it back into the soil. Remember the stories, when the pioneers came across the prairies, of that deep, black soil? That black was carbon. We have been de-carbonizing the soil and putting it up into the air. We can start reversing this by changing the way in which we do agriculture. We can also use different feedstocks. Algae is one of my favorites. You get more oil per acre using these lipid algae than you do growing corn or anything else.

We can also change how we move around. I am increasingly doing talks like this via videoconferencing, using a company called CityIS.[17] I can actually just sit in my pajamas in my home in Colorado and be talking to you and you see the top part of me and the slide show. And no jet fuel. HP has a Halo telepresence and video conferencing system that is almost like being in the same room with people. We are wasting an enormous amount of energy doing things in the old way: $300 billion a year buying and burning energy we do not need to, to deliver services we do want. I am not talking about curtailment; I am talking about being smarter.

> "I am not talking about curtailment; I am talking about being smarter."

And our communities will be healthier if we do this. The typical community is bleeding to death trying to buy energy. Twenty percent of gross income in a community goes to buy energy; 80 percent of those dollars immediately leave the community—this is reverse economic development.

Wes Birdsall years ago put in place a solution. He was the general manager of the Osage (Iowa) Municipal Utilities—hardly the hotbed of industrial innovation in the United States. But he did an interesting thing as a businessperson by stepping across the meter to his customer's side to say, "I'm going to help you use less of my product." Because he realized you do not want kilowatt-hours of electricity, you would not know what to do with one if it walked up and bit you. What you want are the services: cold beer, hot showers, industrial shaft power. He realized if he can get you those services cheaper through efficiency, that is the business to be in. He cut energy bills to half that of the state average and unemployment to half that of the national average because with the lower bills more factories came to town. Per megawatt saved in a community, you will save over

$2 million in increased economic output, over $500,000 in increased wages, and increased jobs.

Van Jones[18] is calling for green collar jobs. Investing in efficiency and renewables will give you ten times the jobs of investing in any central station plant. Renewables and energy efficiency give ten times the number of jobs of investing in coal or nuclear plants. The industries now generate 8.5 million green collar jobs and $1 trillion in revenue. By 2030 such jobs could increase to 40 million and $4.5 trillion in revenues—giving good work to one in four Americans.

Braddock, Pennsylvania, is an example of the green jobs economy. They are a rust-belt town. They went from twenty thousand people down to two thousand. They were dying. Their mayor, John Fetterman, said, "We're not going to die. We are going to attract wind and solar companies." They started growing oil feedstocks for biodiesel on the vacant city land and this kept in place a third-generation, hundred-year-old oil company.

In Sacramento, here in this Central Valley, there are programs to start implementing energy efficiencies, cutting carbon emissions. The Sacramento Sustainability Plan includes:

- By 2030, energy consumption of City facilities will be 25% less than 2005.

- By 2020, reduced carbon dioxide emissions to 1990 levels.

- Work with community partners to reduce the number of "unhealthy," or "hazardous," air quality days by 10 percent.

We can do vastly better. "Agriculture," said Thomas Jefferson, "is our wisest pursuit, because it will in the end contribute most to real wealth, good morals and happiness."[19]

We dream of a future of tract homes and industry in this Valley at our peril. We need to reimagine what the future can be. Remember, our American values stem from small farmers, yeomen farmers, building a democracy. When we begin to do this, you get enormous economic gains. The Republican governor of Florida, Governor Crist, was reading the *Sports Illustrated* swimsuit edition that had a Marlins baseball player standing up to his waist in water, because if climate change goes forward, Florida will flood. So he said, "What would be the cost of implementing climate protection?" And surprise, it is a savings of $28 billion! He convened a Republican task force, they looked at fifty different policy measures, put them all in place, and it saves the state $28 billion.

It is being done here in California. UC Berkeley came out with a study last fall: fully imple-menting AB32, the

"We dream of a future of tract homes and industry in this Valley at our peril. We need to reimagine what the future can be."

carbon cap bill put in place by a Republican governor, will increase state gross product by about $76 billion and will add over 403,000 new jobs to the economy. We can unleash a new energy economy. If we fail to do it, it will be the greatest market failure in history.

Last year around the world we brought on more new wind, 15 GW of new wind, than we ever brought on—even nuclear power back when we were building nukes. A gigawatt is roughly a nuclear-size chunk of electricity. In good sites, wind costs less than just running an existing coal plant. In the south part of the Central Valley, they were bringing on a megawatt a week of solar until the economic collapse. Southern California Edison built a 250-megawatt solar plant on roofs spread around the county at a price point, $875 million, eerily close to the $800 million of a coal plant that was recently cancelled up in Montana. We are nearing what is called "grid parity," where the cost of delivering the services you want from electricity from solar is equal to or cheaper than doing it with fossil plants. And then you get the inevitable question, "But is there a business case?"

Yes, as a matter of fact, there is a very good business case. I call it the integrated bottom line: business manages to profit. You may have heard the phrase "the triple bottom line"—profit, people, and the planet are cost centers to measure organizational success. This is a bit of a tough sell. What constitutes value in a company to shareholders? Profit is clearly part of it, so you take a DuPont that is profitable because it is squeezing out its waste. Another aspect that is driving our profit is innovation. So you take an STMicroelectronics that is driving its innovation because of its commitment to cut carbon. Reduction of risk; remember if the insurance companies won't insure you or your officers and directors? The first lawsuits have started to issue against carbon intensive companies; this is unbooked liability. The sustainable companies are most able to attract and retain the best talent. When they have them, by building green buildings that use less energy, they increase the labor productivity of the people they have got, they enhance market share, they differentiate their brand, they enhance brand equity. They also better manage their supply chain. This helps to explain why Wal-Mart is going green; they are managing their supply chain. Why? Because they are reducing the cost of distrust.

The companies that get it right will be first of the future; we are talking about the billionaires of tomorrow. Let us go back to the first industrial revolution, when we created commerce using water power to make textiles, and then we moved on to steam power and trains, and then electricity and chemicals and cars, and then petrochemicals. Remember the space race? The last wave of innovation gave us all these little devices that carry three thousand songs; who would have thought that we all would have needed three thousand songs in our pocket? Evidently we all do.

But what is next? What is our economy going to be based upon? Are we all going to be burger flippers? I think if we are going to have a dynamic industrial economy in this country, it is going to be what I am talking about: energy efficiency, renewable energy, green technologies. These are the industries in which America still leads.

Bob Willard,[20] consultant to companies, put some real numbers to seven aspects of this integrated bottom line and came out with an enhanced profitability of 38 percent. This is real numbers.

Potential Improvements

1.	Reduced recruiting costs	-1%
2.	Reduced attrition costs	-2%
3.	Increased employee productivity	+10%
4.	Reduced expenses in manufacturing	-5%
5.	Reduced expenses at commercial sites	-20%
6.	Increased revenue - market share	+5%
7.	Lower insurance and borrowing costs	-5%

...yielding a profit increase of +38%

It is no accident that the companies in the Dow Jones Sustainability Index outperform the general market. Goldman Sachs two years ago came out with a study showing that the environmental leaders of the corporate world (companies considered leaders in environmental, social, and government policies) have 25 percent higher stock value than their competitors, and 72 percent of the companies on the list outperformed industry peers.[21]

Richard Florida[22] has shown that regions that protect their environment economically outperform those that do not. The environment of the Great Valley is a critical economic asset that needs to be protected if you are going to have prosperity here in the Valley. A regional blueprint, or I would prefer to call it a "greenprint," provides understanding in how you can encourage local businesses and local vitality. The preservation of rural culture and agriculture, of community within the Valley, and strategies that can be used to enable towns and counties throughout the Valley to prosper are very important tools.

> "Richard Florida has shown that regions that protect their environment economically outperform those that do not."

About a year ago, the Economist Intelligence Unit corroborated the Goldman Sachs finding and found out that the worst-performing companies in the economy are most likely to have nobody in charge of sustainability. A.T. Kearney[23] came out with a study showing that what they call "green winners"—these companies on the Dow Jones Sustainability Index or in the Goldman study—in sixteen out of eighteen industries, businesses deemed "sustainability focused" outperformed their peers over three- to six-month periods and were well protected from value erosion. Remember, this is after the collapse. And they found that the market capitalization difference was about $650 million per company between the green companies and those that had not yet gotten onto it.

How do you get companies to go beyond needing to be penalized? One way is, of course, to use carrots rather than sticks. But be sure that the carrot is actually tasty and not a stick painted orange. The companies that are on the A.T. Kearney study and that Goldman Sachs are tracking have gone so far beyond compliance that compliance is almost no longer relevant to them. In general, these companies are driven by a passionate CEO who understands this almost as a heartfelt passion, not as a regulatory issue. They realize that a corporate commitment to behaving more responsibly is the way that their company will prosper, so they are driving sustainability in every aspect of their company—a very different mental model from "What is the minimum I have to do to get away with it?" So to the extent that we can educate businesspeople in this new way of doing business, in this better way of profiting, we can get away from having to have top-down, nasty sorts of regulation.

There has been some experimentation with performance codes where we invite higher performance and reward it. For example, in California the utilities get paid as much for efficiency as they do for running a power plant. They have some penalties if they do not elicit enough efficiency. This tends to concentrate their mind more to "What are my opportunities over here to help my customers use less?" This totally changed the utility mindset from most utility companies in this country, who are rewarded only if they build and operate central station power plants.

So to what extent can you take your regulations and give companies that go beyond the minimum a reward? If you have green builders in your community, do they go to the head of the queue for permits? This does not cost you anything, but time is money to a builder. Do you have green builder programs where people who want to start building green in a community can start to learn how to do it? Do you have financing mechanisms? Over in Berkeley the city clerk recognized that you can create a special assessment taxing district for essentially anything, typically to do underground wires or clean up an alleyway.[24] The clerk said, "Why don't we do this for solar?" So they created Berkeley FIRST—Financing Initiative for Renewable and Solar Technology. This is a fund of money from Berkeley's sustainable energy financing district that citizens can borrow from, put solar on their roof, and then repay the loan over twenty years through a special assessment on their property tax bills. The property tax shows up only for the affected properties, but not to everybody else. This pilot program sold out in nine minutes; they are going back and doing it again. We put one in place in Boulder County, Colorado, that has $40 million. Palm Desert has done it. There are cities up and down the state. Does your city have this kind of a fund? If companies, residents, can get the funding and have an information source (perhaps your Great Valley Center Energy Primer could be a source) on where to go in your community to get information on efficiency, renewables, how to do it; if their training program is in place for the construction firms that now want to get into the green jobs area—there is a whole array of programs that you can put in place that encourage citizens to become part of the new green economy, rather than regulating.

By the way, watch out for the EPA, which is on the verge of declaring carbon not just a pollutant, which it already has, but finalizing the ruling that it is an endangerment. At that point the EPA will start regulating any significant emission of carbon throughout the entire economy. You might want to start putting

> **"So if you think that global warming is a hoax—well, first of all, the earth doesn't care what you think."**

into place measures to help your businesses deal with this. The threat by the EPA is one of those things driving Congress to put into place national legislation around carbon. So if you think that global warming is a hoax—well, first of all, the earth doesn't care what you think—regulation on that is coming. It is not too soon to start putting programs in place to help your residences, your businesses, your community prosper from this, not just get beat over the head with a stick.

And that brings us to Wal-Mart, which may be the biggest driving force in sustainability now in the entire world. Bentonville, Arkansas—Wal-Mart has pledged to be 100 percent renewable energy, zero waste, carbon neutral, and sell only sustainable products. Wal-Mart! Who would have thought? The evil empire. Here is what they are doing. Doors. They put doors on their refrigerator cabinets and saved about 75 percent of their energy. Then they realized the lights inside the refrigerator cabinets are actually like little heaters, so they switched over to LED lights. And then they said, "Why should the lights be on if nobody is around? Let's put a motion detector on it." So the lights are off unless someone walks up to it. What they had not recognized was that kids love it. They come running up to the cabinet to watch the lights flip on; and where the kids are, the parents are, and Wal-Mart sells more stuff. Trust me, they are not doing this out of the goodness of their hearts.

Here is what Wal-Mart is going to roll out this July 2009. This is the new environmental scorecard. *Energy and Climate:* Wal-Mart seeks to maximize the use of renewable energy and minimize greenhouse gas emissions. *Material Efficiency:* Wal-Mart seeks to maximize efficient use of all materials, close material loops, and minimize waste. *Natural Resources:* Wal-Mart seeks to promote the integrity of nature and a safe, reliable supply of natural resources. *People and Community:* Wal-Mart seeks to promote quality of life and safeguard human health. If you want to sell to Wal-Mart, you will abide by these criteria: energy use and efficiency, greenhouse gas emissions, the use of renewable energy, the efficiency in which you use all resources, waste, recycling, pollution, biodiversity, natural abundance, toxicity, nutrition, livelihoods, and the impact on communities. Last October 2008, they gathered one thousand of their biggest Chinese suppliers together and Lee Scott, then CEO of Wal-Mart, said, "You will meet these criteria if you want to sell to Wal-Mart." This is essentially unprecedented. Wal-Mart, by the way, is the fifth-largest Chinese trading partner; there is the U.S. and the E.U. and Wal-Mart.

They are actually following their own corporate culture. Sam Walton said, "Incrementalism is innovation's worst enemy. We do not want continuous improvement, we want radical change."

> **"Markets are a wonderful servant, they are not such a good master, and they are a terrible religion."**

There is a very important role for government. Companies like Wal-Mart are doing a tremendous amount, but it is kind of like a bad lightbulb joke: "How many economists does it take to screw in a lightbulb? None, the free market will do it." No. Markets are a wonderful servant, they are not such a good master, and they are a terrible religion. We have been confusing that of late.

We are in, if you will, *terra incognita* in economic theory. All of the models upon which our economic thinking has been based are wrong. But if you go back and read Adam Smith,[25] he was very clear that markets allocate scarce resources efficiently in the short term. They were never intended to take care of grandchildren. That is our job. That is the job of a free people coming together in a democracy and saying, "What kind of a future do we want?" And that is your job now. What kind of a Valley do you want?

We—the staff at Natural Capitalism Solutions—wrote a book a few years back called *LASER: Local Action for Sustainable Economic Renewal* in which we encourage a community to inventory its local capital.[26] Now, on a balance sheet, capital consists of money and things. Fine, but we ignore natural and human capital, legal capital, and institutional capital. There are at least nine forms of capital that people who do work in developing countries say are essential to economic prosperity. By inventorying these forms of capital in your community and seeking to enhance all of them in ways that don't detract from any of them, you can begin to have a more civilized conversation about what it is that we want more of.

I am now a professor of a discipline that did not exist when I went to college. The year I graduated from college, the word "sustainability" entered the English language. But I now teach at the Presidio School of Management in San Francisco, in an MBA program in sustainable management, because this is how business has to manage if it is going to be profitable. This fall we are starting an MPA program, Master's in Public Administration. Again, sustainability will be woven throughout the entire curriculum, these principles of what we call "natural capitalism," buying time by using all resources more efficiently, and then redesigning how we make and deliver everything, because the way we are doing it now is unsustainable. And then managing all of our institutions to be restorative of human and natural capital. These are the basis of a durable, competitive advantage.

Natural capitalism is a way of doing business that is more profitable than how we do business now and solves most of the problems that are confronting us, such as climate change and scarcity of water and energy. It is based on three principles. First of all, use all resources dramatically more efficiently, because by squeezing out the waste of resources you put money in your pocket, and it also buys us time to confront the serious challenges facing us. The second principle is to redesign how we make and deliver everything, so that our products are fundamentally sustainable, so that they do not use dangerous materials, they do not harm people or the environment, and they deliver the service that we want in better, smarter ways. The third principle is to manage all of our institutions to be restorative of the forms of capital that we are losing in the way we do business now—particularly human capital (intact communities) and natural capital (intact ecosystems). Both of these are declining. If you look in the Great Valley, we are losing the little towns, we are losing the number of farmers on the land. This is culture that we are losing, it is community that we are losing, it is human capital that we are losing, because of the way in which we now do business. There are a lot of things we can do to regrow community.

This is the sustainability imperative. I do not think you have a choice. Your choice is how do you wish to prosper.

I like this line from *Lord of the Rings*, where Gandalf said, "The rule of no realm is mine. But all worthy things that are in peril as the world now stands, those are my care. And for my part I shall not wholly fail if anything passes through this night that can still grow fair and bear fruit and flower again in the days to come. For I too am a steward, did you not know?"

It does not matter if you are Lee Scott of Wal-Mart or an elected official. And remember, in the end it was the two fun-loving, unassuming little hobbits who took upon their shoulders this awesome task. They were scared, and they did not know where they were going. But in the end, all the kings and warriors and wizards could just stand by as the little people saved the world. I think real leadership is extraordinary courage by ordinary people.

Michael Pollan, in *The Omnivore's Dilemma* and in his latest book as well, addresses it well. Go and read his books, it will give you a whole new sense of the opportunities we have in this country to reinvigorate local farming and deliver healthier food, cut our costs, and enhance our quality of life. The future of this Great Valley is in your hands. It is not fate. There are these drivers of change that are coming at you; those you do not have a choice about. How you respond to them will determine whether or not your children are going to want to live in this Valley, and whether or not people in the United States are going to have food.

This is the only place in all the universe we know of where there is life, and we are the only ones who can take care of it.

So again, thank you very much for caring enough to come to be part of this conversation.

Valley-Wise Living

Things you can do between now and 2020 for a sustainable Valley

1. Use energy efficient lightbulbs. They last about twelve times longer than ordinary bulbs and consume about one-fifth of the energy. They come in all shapes and sizes, including spotlights.

2. Use microwave ovens when possible. They consume 80 percent less electricity than conventional ovens.

3. Wash clothes in cold water. About 90 percent of a clothes washer's energy use goes to heating the water.

4. Enable "power management" on all computers and make sure to turn them off at night. A laptop computer uses up to 90 percent less energy than a bigger desktop model.

5. For maximum dishwasher efficiency, only wash full loads. You can also skip the "dry" cycle—the temperature will be hot enough to air-dry dishes in a jiffy.

6. During the summer, setting your air-conditioning thermostat 5°F higher will save about 10 percent on cooling costs.

7. Air seal and insulate your attic. More than 50 percent of the energy used in a typical American home is for space heating and cooling. Much of that conditioned air escapes through poorly sealed, under-insulated attics. Only 20 percent of homes built before 1980 are well insulated.

8. If your hot water heater is not insulated, get an insulating jacket. Without insulation, water heaters waste about 75 percent of the energy they use. Insulating jackets are not expensive. Buy one that is at least three inches thick.

Resources

Recommended Reports and Books

*Green to Gold: How Smart Companies Use Environmental Strategy to
Innovate, Create Value, and Build Competitive Advantage*
Daniel C. Esty and Andrew S. Winston
Hoboken, NJ: John Wiley and Sons, 2009

*Hot, Flat, and Crowded: Why We Need a Green Revolution—
and How It Can Renew America*
Thomas L. Friedman
New York: Farrar, Straus and Giroux, 2008

*The Green Collar Economy: How One Solution Can Fix
Our Two Biggest Problems*
Van Jones
New York: HarperOne, 2009

"Achieving Sustainability in California's Central Valley"
Mark Lubell, Bret Beheim, Vicken Hillis, and Susan Handy
UC Davis, Sustainable Transportation Center of the Institute of
Transportation Studies, 2009

More on the Web

U.S. Department of Energy, Tips on Saving Energy and Money at Home:
www1.eere.energy.gov/consumer/tips

Flex Your Power: www.fypower.org

Vote Solar Initiative: www.votesolar.org

California Fuel Cell Partnership: www.cafcp.org

California Public Utilities Commission and California Energy Commission:
www.gosolarcalifornia.ca.gov

Food for Thought

Questions for more discussion

1. Who is managing energy consumption in my organization? (Energy efficiency is the low-hanging fruit of the sustainability movement. Designate an energy champion to implement energy saving initiatives for your organization.)

2. How can my organization or business best maintain access, quality, and affordability in a time of diminishing resources?

3. What is the appropriate size and shape of my organization/business going forward?

4. Where should our organization/business grow, or should it?

5. How can traditional and alternative revenue streams be maximized in support of our organization's mission?

Designing the Transportation of the Future

Quentin Kopp

As we look to the future, especially in the area of greenhouse gas emissions, fulfilling mandated state legislation in the reduction of greenhouse gas emissions is directly tied not only to the production of energy, but to the use of transportation. In the last ten years, population in the state has increased by over 11 percent, while vehicle travel has increased 16 percent. Our transportation infrastructure has not really changed much in the last forty years. California's highways, local roadways, and bridges received a D+ grade on the 2006 Infrastructure Report Card, which stated: "As our economy has been expanding and our population has been growing, our investments in the core elements of transportation infrastructure capacity, and operational improvements have not kept pace."[1] It is time that transportation does change and proper capacity is built for the Central Valley's population. As the Highway 99 corridor continues to be developed with improving safety, reducing congestion, and facilitating efficient goods movement as priorities, we also need to be brought from a nineteenth-century train system to a twenty-first-century mode to enhance the movement of people through the Central Valley and connect us to the rest of the state.

High-speed rail (HSR) is an important exemplar, both tangibly and symbolically, of progress in the next decade in the Central Valley and beyond. However, it is not without controversy. According to a fact sheet released by UC Davis's Center for Regional Change, those who support HSR believe it will be a cheap mode of transportation for Californians, with more convenience, cost effectiveness, and environmental safety than other potential methods.[2] For instance, HSR has been shown to consume one-third the energy of an airplane, and one-fifth the energy of the motor vehicle, with current research and development for solar panels directly on the train cars to reduce energy dependency. Judge Kopp in this chapter predicts that high-speed rail cars may generate all the energy they need to operate, possibly by 2020. Others challenge HSR, saying that it is only cost-effective for wealthier populations, who will gain from the financial sacrifices of the poor in funding it. Nevertheless, a state bond was approved in November 2008 for high-speed rail and has gained the approval of California's governor as well as President Obama.

The Honorable Quentin Kopp was appointed to the California High-Speed Rail Authority by the California State Senate and elected its chairman in 2006. Judge Kopp was charged with the task of implementing high-speed train service (200 miles per hour) from Los Angeles to San Francisco. He also serves in the Assigned Judges Program of the California Judicial Council and has been assigned almost continuously to the San Mateo County Superior Court since 2004, with intermittent assignments to the superior courts in Los Angeles, Humboldt, Sonoma, Napa, and Santa Cruz Counties.

Prior to judicial appointment, Judge Kopp practiced trial law in San Francisco and Northern California and was elected to the California State Senate. As an elected local and state legislator for twenty-seven years, he served as a leader on virtually every regional governmental policy-making body affecting the Bay Area, including the Metropolitan Transportation Commission, the Bay Area Rapid Transit Board of Directors, the County Supervisors Association of California, the Golden Gate Bridge Highway and Transportation District, the Bay Area Air Quality Management District, and the San Francisco Bay Conservation and Development Commission. Born in Syracuse, New York, Judge Kopp was educated at Dartmouth College and Harvard Law School and served as a lieutenant in the United States Air Force from 1952 until 1954.

Designing the Transportation of the Future

Transportation, obviously, is not just an important part of the 2020 vision of the future of California, but an important part of the Central Valley of California. As noted before, the demographers forecast that by the year 2030 California—which I think about a week ago was identified as having 38.2 million people according to the State Department of Finance, which makes that calculation on an annual basis in between the ten-year censuses—will have fifty million people. The experts also advise us that California High-Speed Rail (HSR)—"the project," as I will call it—is tantamount in terms of applying a means of transportation to fifty million (plus or minus) Californians by the year 2030, to the need to add three thousand lane miles of freeway plus five runways at major airports, plus about ninety gates. I know that the Central Valley does not have the problem of LAX or SFO or Lindbergh Field or John Wayne Airport, or even the Oakland or San Jose airports…but you try to add runways or freeway lanes in today's climate.

Let me go back to the beginning and come forward as fast as I can. A couple of themes I want to cover are energy and transportation times. High-speed rail is not conventional rail that we think of.

> "High-speed rail is not conventional… nineteenth-century rail."

It is not nineteenth-century rail. Those figures about the amount of time to go from Northern California to Southern California on high-speed rail are

27

substantially accurate. High-speed rail also is not a new technology. Steel wheels on steel tracks have been operating, at a profit, incidentally, for more than forty-four years, beginning in Japan in 1964, in time for the International Olympic Games. High-speed rail operates in revenue service in eleven different countries. After Japan came France with the Train à Grande Vitesse (TGV) system in 1981; Germany with the InterCity Express (ICE) system in 1993; and then Spain a couple of years later. Asia—South Korea, Taiwan, and now China—all have high-speed rail systems. China anticipates and brags that it will have, in two years, three thousand miles of high-speed rail, which I think is unbelievable, but you understand the direction in which China aims to build a transportation system.

High-speed rail is a system today which can operate at 220 miles per hour, and it will do so in the Central Valley with the open spaces that enable it to do so. In congested, densely populated areas like the San Francisco Peninsula, it will logically be limited to 125 miles per hour. But you will be able to travel from Fresno to San Jose, for example, in 65 minutes. You will be able to travel from San Francisco or Oakland to Anaheim in about 2 hours and 58 minutes; San Francisco to downtown Los Angeles's Union Station in 2 hours and 38 minutes.

The single milestone in the development of California High-Speed Rail was last November's (2008) approval of an almost $10 billion general obligation bond issue of the state of California, of which $9 billion is for high-speed rail and $950 million is for entities to connect to high-speed rail, such as the Capitol Corridor, the Altamont Commuter Express, Metrolink in Southern California, and the Bay Area Rapid Transit District in the San Francisco Bay Area. That was a remarkable result in this time—an era of economic vicissitude. The California voters demonstrated a belief in 2020. The weekend before that election, the Field Poll showed us losing with only a 47 percent yes vote, and three days later we prevailed with almost a 53 percent yes vote. When I asked the campaign gurus, "How did we do it?" I was advised that it was voters forty-five years old and younger. I never traveled to Europe until 1982, which is when I first took high-speed rail, and I was fifty-eight years old already. Today people travel in their twenties, thirties, and forties; they know the high-speed rail systems which exist in Europe and Asia.

This project will be almost eight hundred miles, from San Diego in the south to Sacramento in the north. And in so many ways, the Central Valley is the most important part of this project, because you know that the Central Valley suffers from a lack of air service. But high-speed rail in its construction phase over the period between now and the year 2025—when the entire eight hundred miles will be operating for revenue service—will create about 150,000 construction-related jobs, and thereafter 450,000 (plus or minus) permanent new jobs. Obviously, it will enable commuting between the Central Valley and the Bay Area, the Silicon Valley, and Southern California in a way that is comfortable and practical, and less painful than it is today. It will encourage and stimulate businesses to locate in the Central Valley for purposes of perhaps land price and other aspects.

Where we are now in the development of the project: the first phase of the project will be from San Francisco to Anaheim, through San Jose over the Pacheco Pass, through Merced and then down to Fresno, to Bakersfield, past the Tehachapis, to Palmdale and downtown Los Angeles's Union Station, and then to Anaheim, where the Orange County Transportation Authority plans a gigantic new transit center along the lines of Grand Central Station in Manhattan. That phase should start construction section by section in about two years. Within that phase are eight sections: San Francisco to San Jose is a section, San Jose to Merced is a section, and Merced to Fresno is a section.

One of the first sections to open—maybe not the first, but pretty close to it—will be in the Central Valley, between Merced and Bakersfield. We plan our test track to be on that section of the first phase, and the other two candidates are Anaheim to Los Angeles—because the Orange County Transportation Authority contributed about $7 million toward the engineering design last year and again this year—and the San Francisco to San Jose section, because that's the only right-of-way owned by the people of California.

With the approval of the bond last November, we are now in the actual design process and the accompanying required environmental clearance. Our program environmental impact report (EIR) was certified by the Federal Railroad Administration (FRA)—a quasi-partner, in effect, because rail regulations and rail specifications in the United States need change and that means modernization in the manner in which Europe and Asia have accomplished in the last forty-four years. The EIR was certified by the FRA last June (2008) and certified by my board last July (2008).

We are acutely cognizant of grasslands and the national wildlife refuge complex in the San Joaquin Valley. That aspect of the alignment was evaluated, studied, analyzed, and the subject of an EIR not once, but twice, and most recently in 2007 and up until July 2008, at which time the EIR or EIS was certified by our board, selecting the Pacheco Pass as the preferred alignment, preferred over the Altamont Pass. As part of that, we have had the legislature write into law a couple of provisions. One is that there can be no station between Gilroy and Merced, which does not make the mayor of Los Banos happy. Secondly, as part of the mitigation we will spend upwards of $1 million for land preservation so that we can assure interested parties that environmentally, we have mitigated to the extent humanly possible any adverse effects upon the environment between San Jose and Merced. That section is the subject of engineering design, analysis, and public hearings. There will be a draft analysis probably published sometime later this summer (2009), then there will be another round of public scoping before any design is established.

Engineering design is difficult, that is the nitty-gritty of where you go. Do you go on an aerial basis, do you go underground, do you trench? Because one of the acute aspects of HSR is there has never been a single fatality in forty-four years of operation. There were deaths due to the collapse of a pre-WWII bridge in Germany, but not from operation per se. Why? Because high-speed rail runs on dedicated, separated track; no human beings deliberately or carelessly wandering on the right-of-way, no trucks, no other motor vehicles. That means the removal of about 600+ grade crossings between San Francisco and Anaheim just as part of phase 1 of the project itself.

> **"High-speed rail runs on dedicated, separated track; no human beings deliberately or carelessly wandering on the right-of-way, no trucks, no other motor vehicles."**

I am pleased that Sacramento has exhibited interest—particularly the new mayor, Kevin Johnson, is a huge fan of high-speed rail. Here is the way the law is written: a bill that was carried by Assemblywoman Galgiani has a provision—even though the second phase of the project is from Los Angeles to San Diego—allowing engineering work and possibly even construction work to commence in sections of the second phase, including Merced to Sacramento, if those sections are able to generate money without touching the $9 billion bond issue. That is what Mayor Johnson appears to me to be heading to try to accomplish. In other words, if the money is raised locally and regionally, not just from public sources, but from private sources without requiring touching any of that $9 billion, certainly the engineering design can begin and possibly—although not probably—construction could begin before the first phase is completed. The first phase will be completed, all those eight sections, between 2018 and 2020.

The estimated cost of the first phase is, in 2008 dollars, between $32.8 billion and $33.6 billion. How will that be paid for? Well, $9 billion manifestly is our financial foundation. No other state, no other region, with all the talk and discussion under a new presidential administration, is close to California in putting its money where its mouth is. To add to that $9 billion, we expect $2 to $3 billion from local and regional sources—not just public, but also private. Those of you who have seen high-speed rail stations in Europe or Asia probably have remarked about the development which has occurred around those stations. You sell air rights. If you own extra land you sell or lease, long-term, that land for development, and it works financially. Added to that will be $12 to $16 billion in federal grants. And that already, as shown by a new president, is responsible for the fact that in the American Recovery and Reinvestment Act, which he signed on February 17, 2009, there is $8 billion allocated for high-speed and normal rail. California, under the rubric of the governor's office, will submit an application just as soon as the criteria are published by the secretary of Transportation. President Obama's recommended federal budget for fiscal year 2010 includes $1 billion, the first down payment of five years of appropriating $1 billion a year for high-speed rail. In addition to that, the Surface Transportation Act, which is a five-year legislative program that expires presently on September 30, 2009, will be renewed, obviously, for the next five years. And based upon conversations with Senator Carper of Delaware, Senator Kerry of Massachusetts, and Congressman Oberstar of Minnesota, I forecast there will be between $14 and $15 billion over the next five years from the Surface Transportation Act renewal legislation.

As indicated, these systems will operate by electrical power. Someday, maybe by 2020, we will generate all our energy needed to operate. How? Well, right now high-speed rail

"Someday…we will generate all our energy needed to operate."

captures or recaptures about 7 to 8 percent of its energy during the braking process. But there is already research and development on solar panels on the cars, which will enable us to use solar power in the future. High-speed rail consumes one-third the energy of an airplane and one-fifth the energy of a motor vehicle. It is estimated that upon completion of almost the whole eight hundred miles by the year 2025, California's carbon dioxide emissions will be reduced by 12.7 billion tons per year as a result of high-speed rail's operation and there will be a reduction of about twelve million barrels of oil needed—foreign imported oil—for California's transportation purposes.

Finally, let me tell you that I expect that a part of the state of California's application to the American Recovery and Reinvestment Act—that $8 billion—will be money for the construction of our maintenance facility project, which I expect will be in or near Merced, together with a storage yard in the Los Angeles basin and a storage yard in the Bay Area.

"High-speed rail is unquestionably California's future."

High-speed rail is unquestionably California's future. Do not be intimidated by the economy. Remember, Californians built the Golden Gate Bridge during the Depression with general obligation bonds of six counties—including one of the smallest counties in the state, Del Norte County—opening it in 1937. And the state built the Bay Bridge during the middle of that Depression, opening it in 1938. We have never been afraid and we will not be afraid in the future with your continued support.

Valley-Wise Living

Things you can do between now and 2020 for a sustainable Valley

1. Drive less.
   Look into your city's bus routes and bike paths and see if either of these might be a viable option for the trips you usually take in your car. Combine errands.
   Explore the potential of increasing the use of email, video conferencing, and telephones at your workplace to eliminate travel time.

2. If you have to drive your car...
   Learn safe methods drivers can use to reduce fuel consumption in existing vehicles. Visiting a hypermiling website will give you many more tips.
   Choose a car that uses alternative forms of fuel.

3. Think and act locally and regionally with transportation issues.
   Trains, buses, and highways extend beyond a municipality's boundaries, so it is necessary to know organizations and people who work beyond local boundaries on transportation.
   Communicate with your municipality about transportation and become an active participant in your community's transportation planning processes. Join your city's bicycle or pedestrian advisory committee or task force.

Resources

Recommended Reports and Books

High Speed Rail in the U.S.: Super Trains for the Millennium
   Thomas Lynch, ed.
   Amsterdam: Gordon and Breach Science Publishers, 1998

"Route 99 Business Plan," CalTrans, www.dot.ca.gov/dist6/planning/sr99bus

More on the Web

California High-Speed Rail Authority: www.cahighspeedrail.ca.gov

California Transportation Commission: www.catc.ca.gov

Transportation California: www.transportationca.com

California Energy Commission's Consumer Energy Center:
   www.consumerenergycenter.org

Valleyrides.com is a resource available to anyone commuting to and from
   Fresno and Tulare Counties and surrounding communities

Reconnecting America: www.reconnectingamerica.org

TransForm: www.transformca.org

Food for Thought

Questions for more discussion

1. Have (I/we) learned all (I/we) can about California's infrastructure problems and transportation needs?

2. When (I/we) see a problem, have (I/we) found out what level of government has jurisdiction over it? (Sometimes various levels of government deal with different aspects of the same problem.)[3]

A Thriving Agriculture in the Twenty-First Century

A. G. Kawamura

Agriculture in many ways defines the Central Valley and its place and significance in the world order. The Central Valley is one of seven places on our Earth that has this combination of soil, climate, and water that can produce more than four hundred different crops and agricultural products. Of the top ten agricultural producing counties in the nation, seven are in the Central Valley. There is no doubt that this region is an important source of food not only for the U.S., but for the world. However, as Great Valley Center founder Carol Whiteside summarized most effectively, "Agriculture is too often seen as a Third World venture, employing itinerant farmworkers, paying subsistence wages, and taking up space until something better comes along. Nothing could be further from the truth."[1]

With seasonal rainfall unable to support agricultural productivity, state leaders in the 1880s began to develop and promote a series of elaborate plans to irrigate the Valley. Two major systems, the Central Valley Project (federal) and the California Water Project (state), store water in the northern Sacramento Valley and then transport it, through a complex system of canals, south of the Delta. These systems of intertwining canals, dams, reservoirs, and pumps stand as the largest irrigation project ever undertaken in the world. In this chapter, A. G. Kawamura frequently points to an infrastructure issue in our agricultural system, the barriers to a reliable water supply and conveyance system that could assure adequate quality and quantity of water. To him, this is the biggest problem with sustaining agriculture's prominence in California as a global food producer. Having reliable water is just one of the goals of California's Agricultural Vision 2030, a framework for a set of long-term goals for an advanced twenty-first-century food supply.

In 2003, Governor Schwarzenegger appointed A. G. Kawamura secretary of the California Department of Food and Agriculture, a role in which he is dedicated to protecting not only California's agricultural resources, but the environment as well. Secretary Kawamura chairs the Specialty Crop Task Force of the National Association of State Departments of Agriculture (NASDA) and he is a member of the USDA Fruit and Vegetable Industry Advisory Committee and other national committees. On other issues of domestic and international importance, he was an early supporter of renewable energy as well as being a vocal proponent of invasive species prevention, trade promotion, and farm bill reauthorization.

A. G. Kawamura comes from a family that has been involved in agriculture for about a hundred years. His family still grows strawberries, green beans, and other specialty crops in Orange County. A. G. received his bachelor's degree in comparative literature from UC Berkeley and subsequently began a long career in public service to his community and to agriculture. He has become widely known for his passion for education and his commitment to the issues of hunger and nutrition. He has experience outside of agriculture that provides him with the insight to see how agriculture fits into the world order.

A Thriving Agriculture in the Twenty-First Century

Great to be here to talk about the future of agriculture, because ultimately we have to have a future. I think one of the biggest challenges we felt working with the Great Valley Center and working with the Partnership for the San Joaquin Valley over these past years is that California does not have a plan for agriculture as we move decades ahead.

I first want to give a framework of where we are, how we can look at agriculture, and more importantly, how twenty-first-century agriculture is going to fit into California, this country, and globally.

The framework of change is very significant. We have economic challenges. Changes happen very quickly, such as the H1N1 influenza strain that circulated very quickly and appears to be going to a pandemic 6 level. We are very blessed because, while this influenza virus is very virulent, it does not have a very high mortality rate. We are going to have a chance to see what kind of infrastructure globally, nationally, locally, we have in place to deal with something we have been working on for many years. These are the kinds of things that are important: being prepared for the future, recognizing that change is a choice. We have the ability to choose the kinds of changes we want to steer ourselves into our future. Certainly we will have some enormous

> "We have the ability to choose the kinds of changes we want to steer ourselves into our future."

challenges if at the fork in the road we choose not to strategically prepare for some predictable part of our future. If we choose the path that seems laid out, that seems pretty clear where we might head; whether we like that road or recognize we want to go on a different road—this is the time to do that kind of deep thinking.

This is the great work that the Great Valley Center has been doing, in trying to look at the Central Valley and choose a path that we want to see going into the future, whether it is 2020, 2030, 2050, whether it is just next year. These are the important kinds of meetings bringing together a convergence of minds which has to happen to start to make some good informed strategic planning.

> It is just staggering how much potentiality we have with agriculture in our entire state."

We understand that the eight counties of the San Joaquin Valley—if by themselves—would be the number one agricultural producing state in the nation. It is just staggering how much potentiality we have with agriculture in our entire state.

I have had the privilege of being a farmer for a long time in an area that has changed tremendously. Orange County used to be a powerhouse. As a farmer I just want to make an observation, although it should be the same for all businesses, governments, or organizations. When you invest in something, for example when you purchase something on a farm—a new tractor, a new water system, a new variety of a crop—you do so because you are trying to enhance the predictability of your outcome. You are trying to improve your outcome in a predictable way. You buy something, you invest in it (as opposed to a cost), you put it into play, you have studied it enough to make that investment, and that investment, you hope, delivers some kind of predictability in your outcome. We have to take a good hard look in terms of how we are going to look to our future and be wise in the amount of the investment we have, especially if we are going to look at struggling times economically. Then we have to look at new ways to join our resource base and still make those important investments to enhance our predictability.

One of the challenges we have in agriculture, however, is that 2 percent of the American public is engaged in active agriculture; there is a food chain from the farm or field to the table. We talk about 10 percent of the population in California engaged in the food chain, which I think is very true, but in terms of actual production of agricultural products, it is only 2 percent of the public in our country. That 2 percent is constantly trying to define themselves and talk about who they are. But when 98 percent of the folks are busy eating and chewing, the noise sometimes drowns out and mutes the voice of agriculture. The public has an interesting memory; they choose to remember certain myths of agriculture. Some people still think it is the 1940s or 1960s and that DDT is still in use here in this country or in this state. They still continue to look at some groundbreaking, important books, like Rachel Carson's *Silent Spring* or many other books that have come along that talk about agriculture's past practices, but do not understand today's agriculture. But we are not the Midwest, we are California. I recognize that we have to define ourselves in agriculture with the help of many, or we will be defined without our input into the future.

One myth we need to address is that people continue to say that agriculture uses 70 to 80 percent of the developed water in this state. One of the new studies by the Department of Water Resources that just came out recently says 41 percent of water goes to agricultural use, 48 percent goes to protect the environment, and 11 percent goes to the urban centers of the state.[2] When it comes to water, it has been an evolving, improving picture for many years, improving in the sense that the use of water in our state is very widespread. Looking at the last forty years' worth of water use for our state, we have had an increase in actual irrigated acreage, a decrease in the actual amount of water use (14 percent decrease), and yet we have had an 84 percent increase in the value of the crops produced in our state. That is partly why we have been the number one agricultural state over the last fifty years and we are still the number one agricultural state in the country, and that is also why we have over four hundred different crops throughout the whole state. We have this ability to turn water on and off, and that enables us, with a predictable climate, to have an amazing crop mix here in our state. That is a strategic, critical resource advantage that many other places on the planet do not have.

The federal stimulus package supports different ways to give us more flexibility in our water supplies, including underground storage, above-ground storage, and conveyance. That makes people uncomfortable depending upon where you are, or makes people excited depending where you are. The challenge here is that we can take care of the needs of the environment, of the community, down in the Delta especially, and the rest of the communities in the state, if we build flexibility into our system. What we are challenged to do is recognize collectively that if we do not do anything, the predictable outcome is that we are on the third year of a ten-year drought. We will also have a regulatory drought, if you will, because we are protecting environmental species as well. Watch what happens to predictability when suddenly the government says, "We are not going to be giving you any more water," and watch what happens with the rest of the San Joaquin Valley if we move into that kind of horrible situation. We are looking for water solutions statewide over a fifty- to one-hundred-year horizon.

This muted voice of agriculture, or this inability for agriculture to describe itself in twenty-first-century terms, presents us a lot of problems because of the ways we communicate these days, especially with the death of the press. All these new ways to communicate are very exciting and important, such as Twitter and Facebook, but also they basically reflect a new kind of information base that is driven by opinion. We are in jeopardy when opinion starts to drive the policy or the politics of agriculture or other areas.

> "We are blessed…that we can fight over what kind of food should be on the table."

We are blessed in our state and in our country that we can fight over what kind of food should be on the table. We get a lot of choices. We get to choose between organic or conventional, heirloom or genetically engineered. We get to choose between a 365-day supply of some kind of fruit or vegetable that is always there, or a seasonal approach where you only get a locally grown product in its season. We actually have an amazing amount of choices of energy: nuclear, petroleum, biodiesel, ethanol, geothermal, solar, wind. We live in the luxury of abundance where we have an inherent feeling that we get to choose these different things, and we will fight and legislate what kind of food is on our tables.

I had a chance to be in India a couple of months ago to talk at a conference on sustainable global development in the face of global climate change. The reason I was there was because no one was talking about the enormous impacts to agriculture that will take place with global climate change. The simple inconvenient truth of this is that unpredictable weather means unpredictable harvest. For a farmer, the very enormous different specter of unpredictable weather on a giant scale—using Australia as one of the better examples—will tell you that this food supply, this choice that we have, this abundance that we get to choose from, is not really that predictable. It is very vulnerable. In fact, we have to keep a close look at some of our underlying fundamentals that have to be in place to keep agriculture sustainable.

> "We are fighting over what kinds of choices we have and it is a privilege to fight."

We know in this world on any given day there are several billion people that would just like to have something on the plate or turn the light switch on and off at night and have electricity. Yet we are fighting over what kinds of choices we have and it is a privilege to fight. I think it is great that we have the choices and I am very excited about those choices continuing to move forward in this century. But when the choices start to be driven by opinion of what is best, what is right, what is demonized, what is wrong, and you start to see the political process set up by the opinion, that is where we have some very big struggles. The challenge of global climate change is it does not matter whether you are a big farmer or a small farmer, it does not matter what county line, state line, national boundary line; these are all the things that make us a little bit concerned. Such as invasive species and the challenges of watching native species taken over by a species that have been dormant, not a problem, and then suddenly they can leap up and change an entire environment. These are all part of that global climate change scenario that I think fundamentally we have to understand and put into perspective.

We struggle and fight over this abundance and how we are going to have more choices in our stores and in our daily lives. Those of us in agriculture know that by the year 2050 the world population will move up to more than nine billion. At this point the statistics show that we are going to have to double the production of agriculture globally to sustain a Western European kind of diet. Now, I know there is a lot of criticism on how that might happen, and I also know that we could feed the world today and we can continue to feed the world in the future. However, do we have the will to do it? That is a discussion for another panel at another time. Here in our own state we have food deserts, in certain rural and urban areas in our state and in our Valley, where the only diet you have access to is basically a liquor store diet. That is a big challenge for our state, and one of the things we are going to try to move forward as we look to an agriculture vision solution set to deal with some of these problems.

As a backdrop, I want to start with where I see we are today. We have this amazing agricultural system, we have some enormous challenges, and we have a lot of things that we have to pay attention to. One of those things is the fundamental infrastructure that allows agriculture to function well. We have a water problem, we have a drought problem, and we have an infrastructure issue with our system.

Let me tell you a quick story of two countries. Australia is currently in the middle of a ten-year drought. There is a great article in the *National Geographic* that describes Australia, where their agriculture system has collapsed by 50 percent.[3] Can you imagine the San Joaquin Valley agriculture—this enormous powerhouse—shut down by 50 percent? We are three years into our drought. Can you imagine what would happen if we were ten years into a really significant drought? Australia is right now in crisis management—they are mitigating, they are creating desalinization, underground storage, above-ground storage, conservation. They are saying, "You are not going to water your lawn, in fact you do not get a lawn. You do not get a front yard. You cannot wash your car. You are not going to grow rice anymore because we are going to take that water and give it to you guys over here that got grapes. You guys back there are going to have tree fruit crops." The government has taken water rights away. In the fifth, sixth, and seventh year of their drought—as things started to get very, very tough—the government stepped in and took water rights, among other things, away from everybody that thought they had water rights. Now they were wondering if they could just get toilets flushed, if they could just get sanitation to happen. Now they have a whole new system, because they had not built any flexibility into their original system.

In Australia, what used to take ten years to put together—a water desalinization plant—takes three years now because they do not have a choice. They have communities they have had to evacuate and retrain whole populations of people because there is no farming for them to do anymore, and they are moving them out. What we have to recognize is that no matter the date in the future, such as 2016, our challenge is to collectively say we want this to happen by a certain date and let's just go get it done. I hate it when we are driven by the crisis, and we are in the middle of the crisis and having to mitigate, as opposed to recognizing that we have some predictable problems that are going to manifest themselves here very quickly. If this is the third year of a seven-year drought, I guarantee you 2016 is not a bad way to look at it. If we get blessed by rains here in the next couple of years, we may back away mentally and say that we do not really have a problem. We will have an enormous drought here someday that will leave us paralyzed if we have not built more flexibility into the system for the population growth we are expecting.

Ultimately, we will have to have the wisdom and the leadership from all of you who have been a part of all these processes to commit to thriving in the future, as opposed to just hobbling along. California is the eighth-largest economy in the world; we were the fifth-largest just eight or nine years ago. Are we limping towards the eleventh- or twelfth-largest economy in the world, or are we going to move ourselves back toward being one of the powerhouses? Because if we are one of the powerhouses, those choices we talk about, the kind of lifestyle that we all want to have, we will get to have that choice.

> "Ultimately, we will have to…commit to thriving in the future, as opposed to just hobbling along."

The second country I want to talk about is the Netherlands. We had a chance to listen to engineers, who had been helping folks in New Orleans and the Hurricane Katrina area, talk about how to build sea walls and protection from incoming storm surges. Do you remember the pictures of little Dutch kids that were putting their fingers into the levees to hold back the flooding? Those were cartoons that reflected a horrible problem that they had in the 1950s, when they had an enormous North Sea storm surge that basically put their entire country underwater. Now the Netherlands is a country that is 60 percent below sea level. With sea levels rising, you can imagine they have some other issues as well. But these engineers were talking about the sea walls they had put in place. Basically, in the 1950s, after they had that horrible flood with all those deaths, as a country they said, "Never again! Never again are we going to let this happen." They said they have built sea walls that can withstand a one-in-ten-thousand-year storm. We kind of fell off our chairs and said, "You mean one-in-one-thousand, there must be a translation problem here." And they said, "No, no. One-in-ten-thousand-year storm. We have got one-in-one-thousand-, one-in-five-hundred-year sea walls and levees in other places." They knew they were not going to survive the next North Sea storm surge without protecting the main area of the country, so they decided and committed as a country that they were going to thrive and live through it. Now that is the difference between two countries, and the difference I want to put out to all of you.

"We have the ability to decide to thrive or survive."

We have the ability to decide to thrive or survive. That is the line you draw. Surviving is not a good thing. Living and thriving through being strategically minded to invest resources we have in a future that gives us this chance to live and thrive is what this is all about.

When we asked the Dutch engineers about their commitment, there was an absolute concurrence by the population in their country on what kind of future they wanted, because the predictable problem for them was that a storm was going to happen again. The predictable problem for us is that we are going to continue to have droughts and we may see some enormous swings in weather. The predictable problem for us is that we will have population increase and transportation needs.

In California, Governor Schwarzenegger understands infrastructure. As we look at the future of agriculture in our state, and as we look at the future of the state of California with its agricultural presence, those are very important pieces of what we have to have in place. We have to have the fundamental infrastructure that allows us to at least have the ability to turn water on and off. We have to be able to keep the insects and pests out. Eventually we have to have an immigration reform so that we are not afraid of losing our labor on any given day. Those are the kinds of things that can shut down your agricultural system overnight, and the things we are really struggling with during this current drought.

We have been in the process of putting together an agriculture plan, called Ag Vision, which includes what is possible and what is exciting and what is in the future.[4] We worked with a lot of stakeholders, the Great Valley Center, and our State Board of Agriculture to help put together this Ag Vision. We are starting to look at the options. I am excited that maybe when we thought nothing was going to happen and that this economic crisis was just going to bury us, lo and behold there are federal stimulus dollars in a lot of places. We are hoping some of those stimulus dollars really start to help us put together some of those infrastructural pieces that we actually thought we could not fund, but maybe now we will get a chance to utilize.

The Marine Highway that is proposed for the Port of Stockton is a good example. That canal resource has been there for years. Do not forget that California originally sent wheat to China in the 1800s; that was the first major crop that we were growing and exporting. This deep canal enables us to take approximately two million trucks off the road by loading and off-loading at the Port of Stockton. This is a chance to keep a huge amount of trucks off the road between Stockton and Sacramento and the Port of Oakland by putting goods on large barges, moving them back and forth, and utilizing the resources that we are blessed with.

Look at the amazing amount of dairies we have in our state. We are the number one dairy state in the nation. Every piece of manure that comes out of a cow is basically "poop power." We are starting to recognize that there is no such thing as waste coming off any agricultural field. All those things with carbon in it can be converted into an energy product. That will be a great leap forward if all of our dairies, as well as all the other agricultural industries, become able to convert their waste products into valuable energy products. There are coalitions even now working on the renewable energy goals for the country, called "25 by '25," which is by the year 2025, 25 percent of our nation's energy will come from renewable energy sources.

> "We are starting to recognize that there is no such thing as waste coming off any agricultural field."

Wouldn't it be amazing if the San Joaquin Valley, with its enormous portfolio of energy technology capacity—whether it's petroleum, natural gas, geothermal, solar, wind, biomass, dedicated crops that can be grown (drought-tolerant, or salt-tolerant, or any crops)—was energy independent and then exported that energy to the rest of the state?

Can you imagine by the year 2050, if not earlier, every single city on the coast will be pulling water out of the ocean for their water supply? There are certainly going to be technologies that enable us to recognize that we do not globally have a water problem, it just has salt in it. Do we have a water problem, or do we have a salt problem? When we are able to concentrate salt into a brine line—and we already do this in desalination plants—those salts are all valuable minerals, valuable products. If we can figure out how to separate those, package them so they are products, and then the by-products become fresh water, we have the ability someday in the future to be able to have an abundant water source that also supplies a lot of other minerals and other important things that we currently import.

We need to have a convergence among all the diverse kinds of technologies that are out there. I believe in convergence. I believe that parallel efforts to have our state move forward are great, but parallel lines never meet. We have to have a vision of where we want to go, and then converge our resource base towards that vision and a lot of great things start to happen. From the time the Wright brothers first flew at Kitty Hawk to the time we put a man on the moon was sixty-five years or so. We are talking about the condensing of our knowledge base and technologies to increase our ability to really leapfrog into this twenty-first century agriculturally, technologically, engineering-wise, and socially. That is what I think our goal is. In agriculture we think a thriving agriculture base gives us a tremendous platform which allows us to have a lot of different choices and options. Because when we are not worried about where our food supply comes from, it frees us up to have the kind of twenty-first-century society that I think we believe in here in California.

The Department of Agriculture, for example, is putting together the first hydrogen standards on the planet. When the governor said five years ago that we are going to go down the hydrogen highway, many of us cringed. Five or six years ago, hydrogen still looked a little far out there on the edge with hydrogen fuel cells and the rest. But they are already selling and renting cars that have units of hydrogen cells and it is coming along very quickly. Our department has been charged with setting the standards of quality for gas, including safe dispensing; you know when you fill up your gas tank, you see the little seal there and you make sure that you get the right amount of gas all the time. What you see is that we are changing our future because we choose to change it.

I have a friend that has a company that takes plastics and through a catalytic conversion process heats the plastic and drives it back down into crude oil. It is amazing that they can dig up any dump and get the plastics from the dump and put that together and change it back into an energy source. Do you remember the solar reflectors that used to heat your pool or heat your Jacuzzi or your water supply? Some of the new technologies in that arena have figured out to circulate oil in there and heat it up to 500 degrees. That oil can then be used to drive turbines and create electricity. At 500 degrees, most oils begin to break down. What's interesting is that now they have some new technologies where they are using molten salt. Molten salt now can go up to 800+ degrees and they only need to cool it down to 500 degrees to get that differentiation to create and drive these turbines for energy. Now reflector technology in solar paneling is as effective as solar voltaic per square meter. These are giant leaps forward that allow us to look at a different future.

We are already basically stepping into a new era of no-till/low-till activity. Growers, depending on the crop, are moving in that direction. Studies have shown that there are enough yield increases that growers can pretty quickly understand where they are conserving water, or where they are seeing more soil tilth build up, biological activity, within their soil. Transition takes place very quickly once you are able to show a farmer that this is not some new concept that may or may not work. I was a grower, and we were one of the last to transition out of furrow irrigation to sprinklers, then we transitioned from sprinklers to drip irrigation. We were in the forefront in other things that we were doing, but in those arenas I did not have the agricultural background to be out there experimenting with all these different irrigation technologies. But the minute we saw that the guy next door was doing better and was having good results, it was pretty quick when we decided to make that investment to change.

A farmer is always trying to change his odds and enhance the predictability of his outcome. He is always looking at things and studying how he can choose from the smorgasbord of things out there and improve. And when he cannot find things, he innovates. That is always the way for agriculture as it tries to move itself forward, especially in this state.

The difference between living and surviving is a choice. We have to choose to live, we have to choose to thrive, and we have to be able to move forward. Let's go back to the 2 percent of producers of agriculture and the 98 percent of the rest of the public that loves to have the different choices. Our biggest challenge that comes out of our Ag Vision is how to stimulate the 98 percent of the people to be excited and defend the ability to have so many choices of what is on their plate. Right now they do not care, they do not defend it, they do not support it, and they do not see that this system is threatened. It is threatened beyond anything I have seen in my lifetime because of so many chronic amnesia lapses in how we look at infrastructure, how we look at fundamentals, and a lack of a stable platform which we will call sustainability, such as education. The four E's of sustainability are: environmental sensitivity, economic viability, social equity, and education. We need to be able to transfer, maintain, and retain old knowledge with new knowledge and build that up to a steady platform for a society to thrive.

"Do not hesitate to support agriculture."

Those of you who understand agriculture, embrace agriculture, or recognize that it is something that needs help, do not hesitate to step up. Do not hesitate to support agriculture. Recognize that those choices are wonderful to have. And be careful when opinion will drive agriculture into a bad spot for us.

Valley-Wise Living

Things you can do between now and 2020 for a sustainable Valley

1. Get connected with agriculture.
    Shop at local farmers' markets.
    Visit agritourism destinations in the Valley.
    Become a member of a CSA (community supported agriculture), where you buy local, seasonal produce directly from a farmer: www. localharvest.org.

2. Plant a seed.
    Encourage your supermarket or favorite restaurant to source from local growers and support those that do.
    Get involved in local efforts to support and protect farmland, such as California Women for Agriculture.
    Join a local agricultural land trust.

3. Start the education early.
    Help start a garden in your community or at your children's school

Resources

Recommended Reports and Books

Saving American Farmland: What Works
  Julia Freedgood
  Northampton, MA: American Farmland Trust, 1997

"Solid Ground: Land Conservation Models from California's Agricultural Heartland," final report on the Great Valley Center's Agricultural Transactions Program, 2008 (available at www.greatvalley.org)

The Great Central Valley: California's Heartland
  Stephen Johnson, Gerald Haslam, and Robert Dawson
  Berkeley: University of California Press, 1993

Epitaph for a Peach: Four Seasons on My Family Farm
  David Mas Masumoto
  New York: HarperCollins, 1995.

The Omnivore's Dilemma: A Natural History of Four Meals
  Michael Pollan
  New York: Penguin Group, 2006

More on the Web

American Farmland Trust: www.farmland.org

California Association of Winegrape Growers: www.cawg.org

California Certified Farmers' Markets Association: www.cafarmersmarkets.com

California Farm Bureau Federation and local farm bureau chapters: www.cfbf.com

California Farm Water Coalition: www.farmwater.org

Central Valley Land Trusts: www.greatvalley.org/agprograms/ag_landtrusts.aspx

Community Alliance for Family Farmers: www.caff.org

Food Not Lawns International: www.foodnotlawns.net

Land Use, Agriculture, and Housing Work Group of the California Partnership for the San Joaquin Valley: www.sjvpartnership.org (click on Work Groups)

Roots of Change: www.rocfund.org

Rural-Urban Connections Strategy Program (Sacramento region): www.sacog.org/rucs/

Sustainable Agriculture Education: www.sagecenter.org

UC Davis Small Farm Program: www.sfc.ucdavis.edu

UC Sustainable Agriculture Research and Education Program: www.sarep.ucdavis.edu

Valley Land Alliance: www.valleylandalliance.org

Western Growers Association: www.wga.com

Food for Thought

Questions for more discussion

1. How can we provide for a global food system and at the same time give people a feeling of connection to their food and to those who produce it?

2. What are the connections between an innovative and inventive agriculture and other domains of the technology revolution?

3. How do I (or my business or organization) support agriculture's response to new markets, niche markets, and new opportunities?

The Delta's Age of Reason

Jeff Mount

The Sacramento–San Joaquin Delta is the eastern portion of the San Francisco estuary, named for the two rivers that converge there. Locally known simply as "the Delta," it is a web of water channels and man-made islands that stretches nearly fifty miles from Sacramento south to Tracy, and almost twenty-five miles from Antioch east to Stockton.[1] Since the 1950s, California has been pumping water through the Delta for extensive urban and agricultural uses around the state. Fifty percent of the Delta's flows are diverted to 4.5 million acres of farmland and to twenty-three million residents throughout California. The Delta is also a major stopping point for migrating birds and two-thirds of the salmon in California.[2]

Currently, the Delta is ailing and in urgent need of a new management strategy.[3] Salmon and smelt are endangered by human actions and their consequences, such as the pumping system that takes water to farms and urban areas, dams built in place of natural fish ladders, and changing water temperature. Considerable controversy surrounds plans to build a peripheral canal, which "instead of relying on the current labyrinth of earthen levees and channels to flush water from the Sacramento River to giant pumps in the south Delta," would "route water around the Delta from a more northerly section of the Sacramento River."[4] Proponents of this plan argue that it would successfully protect water resources for endangered species of fish and secure water resources currently threatened by crumbling levees for human use. Opponents note that the canal would not actually create any new water and would allow parts of the Delta to return to salt water, ending farming operations in some areas. Water imported into the Valley from the Delta averages close to thirteen hundred tons of salt per day, which could negatively affect surface and groundwater used for various applications, including farming.

In 2009, as the Central Valley begins its third year of drought, it is even more important to understand the Delta system in order to provide the water predictions that are so critical for agriculture and the rest of the economy in the state.

Jeff Mount is an internationally renowned geologist and visionary scientist. He is a leader in research on the Sacramento–San Joaquin Delta and the rivers that lead into it. As a professor at UC Davis and director of the Center for Watershed Sciences, Dr. Mount's research emphasis is on the geomorphic response of lowland river systems to changes in land use and land cover and the links between hydrogeomorphology and riverine ecology. Dr. Mount currently holds the Roy J. Shlemon Endowed Chair in Applied Geosciences at UC Davis. He has worked extensively on the interaction between water resource management and ecosystem management in the Central Valley, Sacramento–San Joaquin Delta, and North Coast of California. His projects include analysis of geomorphology of floodplains, floodplain response to nonstructural flood management measures, development of new floodplain restoration methods, role of hydrologic and sedimentologic residence time in riverine ecosystem health, and development of coupled hydrogeomorphic and ecosystem models for environmental monitoring.

Dr. Mount received a BA in geology from UC Santa Barbara and a PhD in earth sciences from UC Santa Cruz. He is a former member of the State Reclamation Board and a former chair of the California Bay-Delta Authority Independent Science Board, and he is the author of *California Rivers and Streams: The Conflict between Fluvial Process and Land Use*.

The Delta's Age of Reason

I want to talk about the Delta and its implications for what you are talking about here these two days. Instead of my usual Dr. Doom—as described by NPR—talk, I was told to look out ten or eleven years, to 2020. I am going to give you my view of what the world will be like, relative to the Delta, in 2020. I will maintain you have to pay attention to the Delta; you ignore the Delta at your peril, regardless of where you live in the Great Central Valley.

First of all, because I come from a science background, I want to embed some science in all of this. I am going to give you a prediction for 2020 about certain conditions or events that have roughly a fifty-fifty chance or greater of occurring. This is based on analyses that I or my colleagues have done or, in some cases, my best professional judgment.

By 2020 there is a fifty-fifty chance that California writ large will recognize that the hub of the water supply sys-tem is the Delta. I grew up in

"California…will recognize that the hub of the water supply system is the Delta."

Southern California, and to this day I am stunned at how most of Southern California is completely unaware of where their water comes from. People in the Central Valley know where their water comes from, because their livelihood depends on it. But once you leave that Valley you find that the ignorance is limitless when it comes to water. By 2020 there is a fifty-fifty chance they will not be ignorant anymore. Government and the people of the Delta and the Central Valley will know that the Delta is a system which is changing dramatically and rapidly. We will acknowledge by 2020 that what we are doing in the Delta, and those that are dependant upon it, are currently unsustainable. And the conveyance issue, yes the dreaded peripheral canal, will be resolved by that time. We used to refer to it as Voldemort—that which could not be mentioned.

Most people do not realize how important the Delta is to the Central Valley overall. It is the hub of the state's water infrastructure: twenty-six million people get water from it, three million acres are irrigated by it. It is the most important part of the state's water supply system. When it breaks, the state's water supply breaks. My good friend and colleague Jay Lund, professor of environmental engineering, has said that if you want to break the back of California in terms of water supply, you do it at the Delta. It is a system that has utterly transformed, from a seven-hundred-thousand-acre tidal freshwater marsh to a network of about five hundred miles of channels with levees surrounding them and farms and some fairly complex infrastructure.

Subsidence. One of the issues that we will be facing in 2020 is the subsidence that is occurring in the Delta. It has some of the most subsided land anywhere in the world. You have places now in the Delta that approach 25 feet below sea level. This is due primarily to oxidation of the organic rich soils. Subsidence will continue into the Delta because the two largest landowners in the Delta are going to continue to farm: the Department of Water Resources (DWR) and The Nature Conservancy. Farming is going to lead to the loss of roughly 165 million cubic yards of soil in the Delta to the atmosphere through oxidation. You cannot just borrow soil from somebody else in the Delta, you have to go outside the Delta, which costs roughly two to four billion dollars' worth of soil to replace it. That also will add up to, over the course of the next ten years, twenty million tons of carbon into the atmosphere with a rough value of one hundred million dollars in today's market. And of course subsidence will increase the risk of levee failure in this system.

Sea level. You cannot ignore it. The Delta is tied to sea level and sea level is rising. All our recent measurements suggest that it is rising faster, and most projections suggest that it will continue to rise at a faster rate. I do not care what the cause is. All I know is that our empirical evidence suggests that it is rising, and it is rising faster. The current projections are that we will see a rise somewhere between one to two and one-half inches by 2020 and around twelve inches by 2050. That does not sound like much, but when there are eleven hundred miles of levees whose performance is tied to sea level, you have to keep up with the rise. DWR's ballpark estimate is that it will cost $100,000 per inch, per mile in this system, just to keep up with sea level rise. Remember, the levee system is deemed by all to be inadequate for current conditions. Just to bring these levees up to a minimal standard is $1.4 billion. To prepare them for 2050 is at least another $1.5 billion. These are big numbers that cannot be ignored.

The past is a predictor of the future. We are going to see one or more significant floods in the next ten years. We can pretty much count on a significant flood every decade in this system. In fact, this you can bet on. We will almost certainly see one large El Niño event within this system by 2020. El Niño events do not tend to be so bad for the Delta; it is the large floods that are bad. We will also most certainly see a multi-year drought during this time as well, and this is going to produce considerable pressure on this system and will hopefully push us along to some better decision making.

Flooding. Islands are going to flood in the Delta. If you

> **"It is a virtual certainty that by 2020 we will see one or more islands flood."**

go ahead and look at the risk factors for just flooding—there is flooding of the islands associated with either high water from inflows or high tides—it is a virtual certainty that by 2020 we will see one or more islands flood. In fact, there is a roughly fifty-fifty chance we will see seven islands flood. If you have seven islands flood in the Delta, the recovery costs are anywhere from $350 to $700 million. The reason I am focusing on these big-ticket items is that we have to face up to the fact that this is going to get very, very expensive.

I did a commentary in the *Contra Costa Times* with Jay Lund[5] which highlighted the work of one of our students, Robyn Suddeth. She did a marvelous peer-reviewed study of whether it makes economic sense from the perspective of a landowner, business, or the state to reduce risks by upgrading the levees. She looked at the land values and asset values within the Delta and whether or not they should upgrade the levees and/or restore them once they fail. She found that for roughly a quarter of the Delta it does not make economic sense to restore those islands once they fail, which is pretty controversial, especially if you own one of those islands. By 2020, we will finally have gotten our hands around this problem, understood it, and actually have a policy which makes the hard choices of deciding which land we are going to invest in, based on asset and land values, ecological importance, or critical infrastructure. We will prioritize investments in the levees and allow some islands to flood. By the way, my ecologist friends tell me this is not a wipe-out; this may actually be good for the fish that are in trouble.

We are also going to need to come up with alternative economic strategies for the Delta. I work with Peter Moyle, associate director of the Center for Watershed Science at UC Davis. He is a world-class fish squeezer, he loves fish, and he keeps reminding me it is all about fish. It is fish that are playing a major role in the reduction of water exports from the Delta. What does the future hold for them? Well, it is not good. The consensus of the biological community is that probably by 2020 there is a greater than 50 percent chance the delta smelt will go extinct. Do not think for a moment that that solves our problem in the Delta, because waiting right in the wings is long-fin smelt and the Sacramento River salmon, as they suffer from the same hurts the delta smelt do. For this reason, I am saying that we will probably still have the same restrictions on exports in 2020 that we do today based on the Wanger Decision,[6] which is not a happy outcome. By the way, there will be twenty to thirty new invasive species in the Delta; that's the current rate of new invasions that are coming in.

The Delta is an estuary, not a river. Estuaries, by nature, are a little bit salty, some more salty than others. We are currently exporting a great deal of salt out of the Delta and we are leaving it in your Central Valley. The net result of this is that over the course of the next ten years, if we continue average export rates from the Delta, there will be five million metric tons of salt that stays in the Valley. It does not leave, it does not come back through the San Joaquin River, it is a net accumulation of salt. This is the work of Richard Howitt, professor of agricultural and resource economics at UC Davis. His estimates are that aggregate over a ten-year period about $1.2 billion will be lost in agricultural production due to salt accumulation in Valley soils, and that it gets much worse as it goes out into the future. The water of the Delta—what people are fighting about right now in terms of maintaining that water—has got a lot of salt in it and that is going to be a major problem going forward.

The other issue is that there are a lot of people in the Bay Area and Southern California who drink that water. The roughly two million acre-feet of water that is exported annually from the Delta go to the drinking water supply and urban supplies. What has not been talked much about is the costs associated with that. Just to treat this Delta water and to deal with the disinfectant byproducts that cause cancer is $200 million to $1 billion per year. This cost is expected to rise dramatically as the sea level rises and salt intrudes into the Delta. We have to switch over to new types of treatment, so this is actually a low estimate. Metropolitan Water District is aware of this and the Bay Area is aware of this. They do not know quite what to do about it at this point.

Urbanization. I was one of those people freaked out about urbanization when I was a member of the State Reclamation Board. Ten days after Hurricane Katrina, this radical reclamation board I was on dared to ask the question "Is it really a good idea to put all these houses behind these levees?" So we were fired. Yes, I was terminated by the Terminator, and I won't be baaaack. After that, in the typical flurry of legislation that goes on after this—everybody is a hydrologist the day after the flood, and everybody is a geologist the day after the earthquake—the legislature became experts and crafted a series of bills that, much to my shock, the governor actually signed. I believe that one of the unintended consequences of these bills will be a significant reduction in new urban development around the Delta. Developers and cities will not be able to afford to meet the new flood standards. So I think urbanization is going to take care of itself as a problem in the Delta, and by 2020 we will not be seeing a lot of new development in the Delta.

I think the Endangered Species Act (ESA) restrictions on the Delta will continue for another decade. The reasons are several. If the state chooses to do a peripheral canal or a set of peripheral pipes, they will probably not be functional by 2020, because you have to add five years for lawsuits, minimum. Water scarcity costs for the next ten years are going to be very expensive, on the order of two to four billion dollars in scarcity costs. So there has to be an adjustment in thinking. I do not think we are going to get rid of the ESA, at least not under this administration. The ESA is forcing us to face up to things we have not really wanted to talk about in the Delta, and that is that the current use of the Delta, regardless of the way we are managing the species, is not sustainable in the future. On the other hand, the ESA signed by Richard Nixon thirty-five years ago is so inflexible; it makes it really difficult to manage toward a really different future. The ESA is all built around trying to recreate the past in order to keep the species going, but we cannot restore native ecosystems.

So here are my Nostradamus predictions for 2020. And I actually see a change by 2020 in the way we do business.

From 1996 to 2006, we were trapped in what I call the **Age of Indecision.** At that time, we naively believed that if we pumped enough money into the Delta, into science, and into restoration that somehow a miracle would occur and everything would work out. This was the age of "we will all get better together." Instead, we all got worse together during that period of time. During this time a whole lot of money came into California. A tremendous amount did get done, and we did not spend all that money for nothing, but we spent money outside of the Delta, rather than facing the hard choices within the Delta. There were substantial improvements in salmon habitats and fish screening, for example, and the way we managed water outside of the Delta. But the Age of Indecision basically ignored the fundamental problem, so very little was spent within the Delta where the actual major problem really lies. We did not move forward in making the right strategic decision.

Right now we are in the **Age of Absolutes and Absolutely-nots**. People are staking out positions which are absolute and views are all in black-and-white. "We will absolutely not compromise on this: you will absolutely not build a peripheral canal"; "We absolutely must have more water out of the Delta"; etc.

> **"[In] the Age of Reason… there will be compromise and our choices will be based upon logic rather than absolutes."**

The current Age of Absolutes will eventually give way to the **Age of Reason,** when there will be compromise and our choices will be based upon logic rather than absolutes. I am hopeful that during the Age of Reason we will end the use of blogs as the home for science. The blogosphere apparently qualifies for peer review because so many people, many of whom write blogs themselves, read it and believe it. I am also hopeful that at the dawning of the Age of Reason we will remove "quotes," because I have noticed that in the blogosphere if you do not like something you write about it as a "study" with quotes around it, because maybe people will cast doubt on it if there is a "quote" about it.

Will behavior suddenly change in the Age of Reason? I think that reason will prevail after we go through a period of five to seven years of intense litigation and some key issues are resolved. So maybe that is a hopelessly naive way to explain it, as reason will prevail at this point because the courts will have made their decision and we are going to go ahead and do something. I have also found that through time people do eventually, when given enough information, begin to move off the absolutes. We are a long way from that now in the Delta. Other conflicts I have been involved in, they move out of the absolutes eventually into reason.

If that was not depressing enough, let me stimulate some discussion as it relates to the coming Age of Reason. I've been embroiled in a Klamath River controversy; I've been involved in the Delta controversy; I've been involved in a bunch of controversies (maybe they are a controversy because I am involved). In each of these, their own Age of Absolutes tends to be dominated by myths. These myths about the system are used to political advantage. Never mind that facts are the first casualty in these wars. As part of the Age of Absolutes we suffer from too many myths. So here are my top ten myths that will be exploded and defeated by the year 2020.

Myths That Will Disappear During the Delta's Age of Reason

Myth 1: Water that flows to the sea is wasted. Water that flows to the sea is necessary to keep the Delta and the San Francisco Bay alive. If you take out that water, those ecosystems will collapse and eventually the conservationists will come for that water. Water that goes to the sea is anything but wasted, it actually is absolutely necessary for sustaining the very services we expect from these systems.

Myth 2: Most of our water is allocated to the environment. When the flood of 1997 roared through and five hundred thousand cubic feet per second were running down the Yolo Bypass and into the Delta, there was a belief that somehow that water was allocated to the environment. That is the kind of shady accounting that will not survive close scrutiny.

Myth 3: Groundwater is separate from surface water. Groundwater is not separate from surface water, except by lawyers. Scientists do not separate it. You do not really separate it; you just do not want anybody to connect the two, because of the consequences that might occur. Groundwater is intimately connected with surface water and will be regulated as such.

Myth 4: Conservation can solve our/their water problems. **People think** that if people who grow crops would conserve water, that would take care of all our problems. Again, this is a complete myth. We cannot conserve our way out of this problem. This myth typically derives from a failure to understand applied water and consumptive use of water and the market forces that drive agriculture. No, to significantly reduce agricultural consumptive use, you will have to retire some land. Conservation is not a silver bullet.

Myth 5: Desalinization can solve our/their water problems. **Desalinization** is the hoped-for technology that will somehow take care of everything. In the blogosphere it is frequent to see "Desalinization will solve everything." No. Desalinization is an energy hog and we are past peak oil, so I do not think that is going to solve our problem by 2020.

Myth 6: The peripheral canal is a Southern California water grab. **I want** to remind you that out of the six million acre-feet of water that are exported from the Delta, four million go to the San Joaquin and Tulare Basin, one million go to Southern California, and one million go to the Bay Area. The only difference between Southern California and the Bay Area in their use of the Delta water is the Bay Area returns it to the Delta as sewage effluent.

Myth 7: Water markets will solve the Central Valley's problems. **Even economists** will tell you water markets are not going to solve our problem. You cannot solve this existing problem simply by buying and selling and trading water. Improving our ability to trade and move water will help a great deal, but it will not be the silver bullet solution. Unfortunately, there are people in the legislature who believe this myth to be true.

Myth 8: We can restore native ecosystems. **No we cannot. They are gone.** These are naturalized systems, full of invasive species. Ninety percent or more of the biomass in the Delta today is non-native. Ten percent of it is actually native biomass. At the same time, the land of the Delta is being exported into the atmosphere as its soils oxidize. The Delta is a hole in the ground: eight thousand Rose Bowls' worth of a hole in the ground that you cannot fill back up. What we can do is manage for key attributes of those ecosystems which support desirable species, but we can't recreate native ecosystems. And the ecosystems of the future will be very different than those of today. There is no restoring the Delta.

Myth 9: Fix the levees and reduce exports and everything will be fine in the Delta. **This myth completely ignores the complexity and reality of the present,** where business as usual is bad business, and denies the reality of the future. This is a strategy based on hope and little else.

Myth 10: More surface storage will solve the problem of (preconceived notion here). Whatever preconceived notion you have about water in California, it will not be solved by more surface storage. I am yet to be convinced that more storage is necessary in this system, or even cost-effective. This is the big one we are going to fight about between now and 2020.

Bonus Myth: Because of climate change, we must (preconceived notion here). All preconceived notions about what we should do can somehow be tied to climate change, whether you believe it is happening or not. It is one of the things I have noticed, especially in dealing with the legislature. Whenever they say, "We have to do something!" then, whatever that something is, it is followed by "because of climate change." Beware the linking of preconceived notions and their solutions to climate change. Roger Bales, professor of hydrology at UC Merced, is doing some of the best work on climate change within this system, and he will tell you there is still going to be water in this system, it is just going to come a little earlier in the year. We are still going to have agriculture in this Valley, it is just going to be a little different. It is not the doomsday world that I am so famous, personally, for delivering.

Regarding those fifty-fifty predictions that I have just presented…I am off the hook if there is an earthquake. Because there is less than a fifty-fifty chance of an earthquake by 2020, I did not include it in this prognostication. If there is a major quake, all of everything I just said does not pan out. I have just hedged my bets.

Everything I have said to you today, with the exception of the earthquake, I believe has greater than a fifty-fifty chance of happening. Because it is greater than a fifty-fifty chance, it does not mean that it actually has to happen; there is still a probability that it might not happen. Some of these difficult issues that I have raised, particularly scarcity costs associated with water and the salt aspects, we actually can manage if we choose to.

But we are at a political moment which is so important and fragile right now, with the Bay-Delta Conservation Plan, the state legislature going to go nuts with a special session on water, the governor wanting to do something before he leaves office, and Senator Feinstein wanting to do something before she leaves office. All of these are aligned together. Now is the time to actually do something about it. I am quite optimistic that we are headed in the direction of taking a regional approach to water. We have been moving in that direction for the last decade. There are integrated regional water planning processes that are going on today that look quite promising. The localization of water and water management is going to be a thing of the past. This is really a regional problem.

I do see two things that are for sure in 2020: the Delta Protection Commission and the Delta Conservancy. The commission is strong and has the ability to appeal land-use decisions and use their clout. I see a Delta Conservancy which takes on the jobs of ecosystem restoration, land acquisition, and land management. I also see some kind of overarching group which sets up a plan. How that plan for the Delta is then translated to the federal government, the state government, the counties, the local governments, the two hundred different agencies that have jurisdiction over part of the Delta—I am completely unclear on that. But we are going to need some kind of umbrella plan for the Delta that compels people to cooperate with it. I do not see any other way; otherwise we are back to where we were for the last hundred and fifty years for the Delta, which is not working out so hot.

> **"We need to make a strategic decision about the peripheral canal, sometime before 2020."**

Finally, we need to make a strategic decision about the peripheral canal, sometime before 2020. I try very hard not to let my own personal biases creep into my analyses and to remain as neutral on these issues as possible. Despite the view of some, including the press, I am agnostic on the canal. Yet we need to make a decision. This decision has huge economic, environmental, and societal costs and benefits associated with it. But once that decision has been made, then we can begin to sort the rest out. I am not telling you which decision you should make, I am just telling you you've got to make a decision. If we could just get off the dime and do that, I think we would be better off.

Valley-Wise Living

Things you can do between now and 2020 for a sustainable Valley

1. If your shower fills a one-gallon bucket in less than twenty seconds, replace the showerhead with a water-efficient model.

2. Put food coloring in your toilet tank. If it seeps into the toilet bowl without flushing, you have a leak. Fixing it can save up to one thousand gallons a month.

3. Use a commercial car wash that recycles water.

4. Consider replacing part of your yard with native plants that require less water. Or next time you add or replace a flower or shrub, choose a low-water-use plant.

5. UC Davis Arboretum All-Stars is a list of plants selected specifically for Valley gardening. You can also do a search by water needs and find plants for drought resistant gardening: http://arboretum.ucdavis.edu/valleywise_gardening.aspx.

6. When washing dishes by hand, don't let the water run while rinsing. Fill one sink with wash water and the other with rinse water.

7. Compost vegetable food waste instead of using the garbage disposal, and save gallons every time.

8. Adjust your watering schedule each month to match seasonal weather conditions and landscape requirements. And don't water your sidewalk.

Resources

Recommended Books

Unquenchable: America's Water Crisis and What to Do About It
   Robert Glennon
   Washington, DC: Island Press, 2009

Introduction to Water in California
   by David Carle
   Berkeley: UC Press, 2009

KVPT Public Television's documentaries *Salt of the Earth* and *Liquid Assets: Our Water Infrastructure*

More on the Web

University of California, Davis, Center for Watershed Sciences: watershed.ucdavis.edu

California Department of Water Resources: www.water.ca.gov

The Nature Conservancy: www.nature.org

Delta Protection Commission: www.delta.ca.gov

Bay-Delta Conservation Plan, at California Natural Resources Agency: resources.ca.gov/bdcp

Community Water Center, Visalia: www.communitywatercenter.org

San Luis and Delta-Mendota Water Authority: www.sldmwa.org

Water—Use It Wisely: www.wateruseitwisely.com

H_2O Conserve: www.h2oconserve.org

Clean Water Action: www.cleanwateraction.org

Planning and Conservation League, Investment Strategy for California Water: www.pcl.org

Water Education Foundation: www.watereducation.org

Food for Thought

Questions for more discussion

1. Does my city meter residential water use? Why or why not?

2. How does water use in the Central Valley compare with other areas of the country?

3. To what degree should preservation of species take precedence over water for farming?

A Community Approach to Health and Health Care

Richard Pan

The Central Valley faces significant health issues. Asthma rates, obesity, access to care, ratios of specialty physicians to the population, and the amount of primary care being delivered by emergency rooms all indicate we may be heading toward even bigger problems. If the rate of obesity for adolescents—21 percent—remains the same, in the year 2020 more than one-third of a million twelve- to nineteen-year-olds will be considered obese in the Central Valley.[1] Obesity is just one example of a health consequence spurred by many different factors, including individual health choices but also the physical environment and the availability of support for making the right choices in life.

Access to health care is a huge challenge for the region. While the number of physicians in the Central Valley is slightly higher than the state average, there is still less than one physician available per one thousand Valley residents, a rate that, given the same rate of change seen in recent years, will not improve by the year 2020. But a lack of physicians to care for our citizens does not have quite the impact that it could, when so many people are uninsured and likely do not even visit a doctor on a regular basis. If the percentage of uninsured people in the Central Valley stayed at 2007 levels, their numbers would jump to more than one million with the expected population rise. Fred Myer, executive director of medical education and academic planning at UC Merced, is optimistic about the region's health-care problems:

> We do have the capability, the technology, and the ability to do workforce development to solve these problems…It will take resources, both financial and human resources, but in many ways if we do apply it intelligently, not only can we catch up, but we may be able to surpass the rest of the country in some of these key health areas because the…Central Valley has that type of grassroots enthusiasm to do that.[2]

The Great Valley Center truly believes that health indicators can be improved by fostering partnerships between agencies and residents to improve the basic understanding of health issues in diverse communities.

In this chapter, Richard Pan takes a holistic look at many different types of environments, such as social and physical, and how they contribute to key health disparities. According to Sophia Pagoulatos, a planner for the city of Fresno, there is a critical nexus linking how the "built environment affects human behavior, and then that human behavior can affect health."[3] Among other things, residents of the Valley can help tackle public health issues by improving the quality of their built environment. As the Central Valley moves into the future, now is the time to explore and address the barriers to increasing health access and disease prevention in our region.

Dr. Richard Pan is a pediatrician at the Center for Health Services Research in Primary Care at the UC Davis Children's Hospital. Dr. Pan practices general pediatrics with a focus on helping families with children who have behavioral and learning problems. With specialty training in developmental and community-based pediatrics, Dr. Pan founded Communities and Physicians Together (CPT), a partnership between the University of California-Davis Health System and ten Sacramento-area community organizations, to train pediatricians in creating community partnerships in order to have a larger and deeper impact as child advocates. His most recent research includes issues such as diversity and women in the pediatric workforce and the effective use of tobacco taxes.

Dr. Pan received his Medical Doctorate from the University of Pittsburgh School of Medicine, his master's in public health from the Harvard University School of Public Health, and his bachelor's from Johns Hopkins University and performed his residency at Massachusetts General Hospital in Boston.

A Community Approach to Health and Health Care

The question is, "Will we be healthy in the Great Valley in the year 2020?" Our president has indicated that health-care reform is one of his top priorities. But is it health-care reform we want, or is it health reform we want? Certainly, health care is very important. But in the end, what we want to really think about is what drives health. It is not what kind of health care I get that I really care about, it is how healthy I am.

As we try to look to the year 2020, I am going to go over some statistics. We have some good trends, and we have some not-so-good trends. One of the good trends is that since 1900, the U.S. life expectancy has been increasing; we have been living longer.[4] There are some concerns that with obesity that may change for the first time in over a century, but hopefully that will not happen.

We have made tremendous successes over the past century in many areas. If you look at heart disease and strokes as the first and third leading causes of death (age-adjusted death rates),[5] you see that we have been able to make significant strides in what has led to death in many different arenas. In fact, because of our success there are now increased rises in things such as Alzheimer's disease, kidney disease, and Parkinson's disease. This is actually a story of success, of our ability to provide acute care and intervention care for some of our leading killers. In fact, malignant neoplasms (cancer) are actually starting to trend down recently. So again, for what we have been able to do, we have made marked changes in the leading causes of death.

This is tied to access to health care in many cases, which is a challenge here in the Central Valley.

However, in order to achieve some of these things, we have had to spend a lot of money. The national health expenditure is currently driving the health-care debate, as the expense of health care increases. National health expenditure is about 16 percent of the Gross Domestic Product.[6] People are projecting that our health care expenditures will reach 20 percent. It was not that long ago, in the 1990s, when people said it would be totally unsustainable if we passed 15 or 16 percent, which is where we are right now. There is a lot of concern about whether we are spending our dollars most effectively. When we compare ourselves to other countries, we are spending two to three times as much on health care per person and not showing overall health outcomes that are significantly better. Often, many times, our outcomes are far worse than in other countries.

Our current system of employment-based coverage is declining as well.[7] With the increased rise in health-care expenditures, businesses are finding it harder and harder to provide this kind of benefit. Employers are reducing health-care coverage because of the expense, in order to keep their businesses afloat. Where are we spending all that money? The top three rising costs are: hospital care, physician and clinical service, and prescription drugs. Public health costs can barely be seen on the graph. For all the money that we spend, we do not spend very much on prevention. Even though we are spending much more now for these other things and the rate of rise is very steep, the rate of rise for public health is pretty flat and may probably be going down. We are not making those investments in prevention; we are paying for acute care, paying for when the big things happen, but we are not trying to prevent them. That is an expensive way of approaching health.

I have been asked to address what may happen in 2020. The easiest thing I could do is take those trend lines and project them out: in 2020 we will live longer and we will see continuing declines as we improve in terms of heart disease and cancers. We will see more diseases of the elderly, and we are going to make advances in neuroscience.

"The past is not the predictor of the future. The future is dependent on all of us."

The past is not the predictor of the future. The future is dependent on all of us. I cannot really predict what will happen in 2020 because it depends on what all of us will do. Will we make those investments in prevention? Will we change the way we build our infrastructure? Will we look at taking different approaches to health, not just health care, that will change our demand on health care and need for health care? Will we restructure the way we do health care? Ask yourselves: What are you willing to do? What are you willing to try to advocate for in order to improve health in the Central Valley?

To give you a framework for thinking about what we can do to try to improve health in the Central Valley, I will refer to a diagram from a book called *Why Are Some People Healthy and Others Not?*[8] This book was written by a group of epidemiologists in Canada who took a look at the epidemiological data and created a construct for looking at the drivers of health in a population. At the top is your *social environment*—the environment in which you live in terms of your interactions with people. Are you in a place where you feel supported, where you have connections with people, or are you isolated and without any connections, or do you feel stressed or threatened all the time, living in an unsafe environment? Another factor is your *physical environment.* Do you have housing? Your *genetic endowment* certainly has an influence as well. Those factors all combine and then lead to *individual responses* that are either biological, behavioral, or both. Those individual responses can lead to *disease*, which is what the traditional *health-care* realm addresses. So when you get sick and you have something called a disease, you go to a doctor or some other provider, and they try to deliver health care to ameliorate that. But in the meantime those responses also impact your *well-being* and your *prosperity*, and your prosperity also impacts your well-being. That modulates your individual response in the sense that if you are feeling pretty good and life is going pretty well, when that same stressor hits you, you will react to it very differently than if you are already under a tremendous amount of stress, having a lot of different problems going on.

The Healthy People 2010 Determinants of Health diagram shows many of the same elements: *physical* and *social* environments affecting *behavior* or *biology* response impacting an individual. And then that modulates *access to quality health care* and *policies and interventions,* in terms of what kinds of things we do to affect our environment.

How much does health care really contribute to health?

When people try to do calculations on health, it turns out that 10 to 20

"How much does health care really contribute to health?"

percent of your health is influenced by your access to health care. Certainly, access is a very important element. If you had a heart attack or stroke or you got hit by a car, you would definitely want your health care to be there. But as far as your overall health, more important pieces are your behavior patterns (40 percent), many of them often set during childhood; genetic predisposition (30 percent); social circumstances (15 percent); and environmental exposure (5 percent).[9] There is going to be some variation, but this is approximately where it is. If we want to think about how to make people healthier, we have to think about behavior patterns that we are creating in terms of environment, what the social circumstances are that we create—basically, what kind of society we are creating, as well as the environmental exposures, and genetics, because that is also modulated by our environment.

For example, there was a famous study done in Britain called the Whitehall II study. Researchers studied bureaucrats in the British civil service because they technically had equal access to health care; they all get the same health-care benefits. Because they were all working for the government, the researchers could survey them and make them answer the surveys (researchers love that kind of population because you can collect all the data you want on them) and then adjust the data for the access to health care. The participants were asked about their general health, mental health, physical performance, and disability. The administrators, the people who were in charge of the departments, were considered the high grade; the middle grade was the middle managers, and the low grade was the people at the front desk, such as the clerical staff. Generally, the lower grade you are, the more likely you are to have health problems, and you rate your health worse. The researchers have correlated this with the level of control you have over your environment. People at the top can control things and make decisions over their environment. People at the bottom are being told what to do and do not feel like they have control. In fact, physiological studies which researched stress hormone levels found that people who are in the lower class of the bureaucracy have chronically higher stress levels and other physiological measures indicating higher risk disease states. This is showing you the impact of social structure and class in relation to health. They all had the same access to health care, so that was not a variable that was different.

I want to also talk about the principle of risk-reduction health promotion. Our life is on a developmental trajectory in terms of health. We talk about health not just as a point in time; your health is based on what happened to you before as well. There is considerable evidence that health in childhood has tremendous influence on health later on. One example of that is obesity, one of the leading public health measures. There are several preliminary studies that show that if you were ever obese in your first two years of life, your risk of obesity in adulthood is impacted—no matter what happened in between. You could have gotten your weight down: you could be an obese baby, get your weight down through your middle childhood, your teens, early adulthood, and then you will still have higher risk for obesity later on.

The developmental trajectory approach to health shows that things that happen to you translate over time, and risks impact throughout different periods of your life. There are risk factors that could decrease your health trajectory which could be ameliorated through risk-reduction strategies. For example, you have health promotion strategies to reduce the risks associated with smoking. The help of these strategies can hopefully bring people to their optimal health. When we think about health we need to acknowledge this trajectory in people's life course in their health.

There are things that can happen in your early childhood, or even in your teenage years, that may not show up as a health risk until later. One example is people living with high particulate pollution. As a child, if you live near a highway and are exposed to particulate pollution, you actually develop less lung capacity. We all have excess lung capacity when we hit our early adulthood, when our lungs are maximally developed, but if you have less lung capacity when you are in your twenties, you are more likely to get emphysema in life later on; you will develop emphysema at an earlier age because you do not have as much lung capacity. It may look like this child who is exposed to highway particulate pollution looks just the same as anyone else—they look equally healthy, they're breathing fine—but they are more likely to get emphysema ten years earlier because they have decreased lung capacity. We have to think about these risk factors and how they translate into effects much later on.

The other concept I want to introduce is the idea that there are actually critical periods within the life span. An exposure is not the same no matter when it happens in your life; there may be particular points in your development that have a much bigger impact than others. One example we use in pediatrics is children who have cataracts when they are born. There is a window of about a year to fix that cataract. If someone does not pick it up and notice it, does not take that cataract out before a year, if the surgery is done when the child is two years old, the child will still be blind. The eyes will work, but the part of the brain that had to develop to interpret that signal never developed, because the visual signal did not get in during a critical developmental time. There are these critical periods of time when you need to intervene, and if you miss that window you really have a much harder time trying to correct it, or you may not be able to correct it and have to do a work-around. Entry into child care and entry into preschool are two important critical times.

There is also the concept of intergenerational or multigenerational impacts on health.[10] There are intergenerational effects between grandparents, parents, and children. How do we try to promote positive environments that can help these intergenerational impacts? For example, we know that children, particularly teens, who have at least one adult they can connect with are much more resilient than children who do not. Ideally it is their parent, but even if it is not their parent, just some adult they can connect to, the outcome will be much better than for a teenager who has no adult to turn to. Again, that addresses the social environment and the impact on their health.

Obesity has huge health-care implications. Obesity can be used as an example of looking at how we try to improve health. A study looked at the price of obesity and they calculated that the direct and indirect costs of obesity in California in the year 2000 were probably about $21 billion.[11] That is about half of our state budget deficit, right? Health has huge implications and some of that includes direct costs from increased costs of health care, and some of that includes indirect costs in terms of costs to society. If we are going to look at obesity as a health-care issue, we would say we need more obesity clinics and more surgeons to do bariatric surgery. But if we want to try to truly address obesity, we need to look at the environment.

The link between childhood obesity and adult obesity has been demonstrated by a review of the literature of obesity and preventing childhood obesity done by the Institute of Medicine.[12] Fundamentally, obesity occurs if you are eating too much and not exercising enough. It is easy for some people to think that it is your personal responsibility and you are just not doing the right things; you need to exercise more and eat less. That would be the simplistic answer, but what the researchers recognized is that actually, obesity is influenced by many things: 1) food and beverage intake, 2) physical activity, 3) genetic, psychosocial, and other personal factors, 4) behavioral settings at home, school, and community, and 5) social norms and values. Settings include what kind of food is available and accessible and the quality of that food. Social norms could include everyone getting together at McDonald's as a social gathering place and eating together. Does that mean you stop going to McDonald's? Where is the grocery store; is it accessible? Where can I exercise; is it safe to go into the park? Also included in the framework for understanding obesity in children and youth are primary and secondary leverage points: 1) food and agriculture, 2) education, 3) media—what kind of messages the media is sending you, 4) government, 5) public health, 6) health care, 7) land use and transportation, 8) leisure, and 9) recreation.

We know that watching TV increases the rate of obesity. Researchers first thought it was because you just sat there and decreased your physical activity, but now they think that as a result of watching all the food commercials, you get up and eat more. So how do we really address obesity? We could sit there and shake our fingers at people and lecture them about eating less and exercising more, but we have to recognize that there is this larger social context. How do we create the environment to support people in actually doing the things that we want them to do? I teach our residents that they do not just tell people to exercise; they need to ask them where they would exercise if they could, and that answer is always very enlightening.

Research has also been done on the built environment and obesity.[13] They found that there is tremendous inequality in the built environment which underlies key health disparities in physical activity and obesity. People who are poor tend to live in places where they do not have access to facilities. They were able to map this showing the respondents and their geographic accessibility to schools and recreation facilities. We need to look at communities and how we do land use, because if we are really going to try to address obesity and many other health issues, we need to look at how these factors impact all sorts of different communities.

I would be lacking to present at the Great Valley Center conference without mentioning their report that came out last year on health, which I think is an excellent report.[14] There is an abundance of wonderful data on the Great Central Valley. I am not going to reiterate everything here, but I did want to point out the five recommendations. None of them really say we need more health care, which I think is very wise. The first recommendation is to invest in culturally and linguistically appropriate prevention and health education. The second is to continue to stress healthy lifestyles in youth; again, trying to get down that right life-course trajectory. The third is to reduce poverty. Poverty is a huge driver on health. Poverty is not just a social issue, it is a health issue. The fourth is to develop regional coalitions to improve the environment, because we need to come together and think about how we want to create that environment, both physical and social. And lastly, we need to invest in gathering local data, because if we do not have the data, we do not know where we are going; we will not know whether what we did made a difference or not.

> "Poverty is not just a social issue, it is a health issue."

Some people have argued that the reason some people are poor is because they have poor health; that poor health leads to poverty. Researchers have studied this, and it actually turns out that it is poverty that drives poor health more than the other way around. Certainly, having a chronic illness or having a problem has you less likely to be economically productive, but the predominant evidence indicates that poor health in impoverished populations has more to do with the poverty than that they ended up being impoverished because of poor health.

When we talk about health-care costs going up, it is not just about spending more money, it is actually about changing the way we do things in health care. We need to think about this concept of a "medical home." Right now we have a system that is designed to take care of acute events, so if you have a heart attack or get into a car accident, we jump all over you. The problem is that we now have a situation where a lot more people are living with chronic illnesses and we are not really focusing on prevention. What we do is ignore them until they crash and show up in the hospital and then we dump lots of resources on them, things go well, they leave the hospital, and we ignore them again. This is not a very effective and efficient use of resources. A medical home is the idea that someone would have a primary care provider, a physician, who would coordinate their care, provide ongoing monitoring, and get payment for doing that ongoing care that is not just tied to showing up at the office or needing them at the hospital. A review article of international and within-nation studies has shown that a relationship with a medical home (which is actually about the relationship between the patient and the provider—having that relationship of trust and that longitudinal relationship) allows better health on both the individual and population levels.[15] Also, overall costs of care are lower and disparities of health between socially disadvantaged sub-populations and socially advantaged populations are reduced.

Health care, in spite of the fact you are shown lots of national data, is a very local phenomenon.

The Central Valley is doing relatively well in California in terms of keeping our costs down, because of our ratio of primary care and specialty care, unlike Los Angeles, which has very high costs for health-care expenditures because of a larger capacity. As we think about increasing capacity for health care, which is important here in the Valley, we want to do it in the right way. We want to structure our health-care delivery system in a way that makes sense and not just expand the current model.

The epidemiologists at the Centers for Disease Control also recognize the importance of community health. They developed a model called the Community Guide.[16] Looking at social environment and health, they have also included *health determinants,* such as the importance of equity and social justice, societal resources (human, social, and financial), and the physical environment. The health determinants contribute to *intermediate outcomes,* which include: neighborhood living conditions; opportunities for learning and developing capacity; community development and employment opportunities; prevailing community norms, customs, and processes; social cohesion, civic engagement, and collective efficacy; health promotion, disease and injury prevention, and health care. You have to get all the way to the bottom of their list before they start talking about health care. That is what leads to health outcomes and a level of community health. Studies show how these all connect; it is not just a concept, there is an evidence base behind this.

Here are some examples of groups and activities that are trying to address some of these issues.

Healthy Kids, Healthy Future is a regional children's health initiative (CHI) in the Sacramento region that I chair. We now cover five counties. We have come together to make sure every child in the Sierra–Sacramento Valley area will have access to comprehensive, affordable, and continuous health coverage and a medical home that is culturally and linguistically appropriate. This addresses that first step about access to health care and is making sure there is access to health care for every child. There are other CHIs up and down the Valley, although I know parts of the Central Valley do not have CHIs, such as Stanislaus and Madera Counties. Trying to get access to health care for children is particularly important because there are opportunities to provide prevention and intervention counseling.

Communities and Physicians Together (CPT) is a partnership between the UC Davis health system and ten community partners that started about nine years ago. We send our resident physicians—people who graduated from medical school and are now training in a particular specialty—to partner with community partners to learn about health. We talk to our future physicians about the importance of the environment and the community to health. As physicians, when we train we spend a lot of time in hospitals and in doctors' offices and clinics, and it is very easy to start thinking that when we talk to our patients, that is who they are—the people we see in the hospital and clinic. All of us should know from our personal experiences that the hospital is not where we live and it is not the normal environment. When doctors give you instructions, they sometimes do not make sense because they do not consider the environment you are taking them back into. We want to make sure our residents know what is going on in the community, and not only that, but understand these determinants of health and look at how they can be assets for the communities to improve their health. The residents do this as people who are knowledgeable about health care and about some health issues, but they are not the person in charge, not the expert in the community. They figure out they can partner with the community to improve health care and actually improve health in those communities. This program has been very successful: we have gotten a couple of national awards and we are now encompassing all of the primary residencies at UC Davis (pediatrics, family medicine, and internal medicine). Our community partners have found it particularly valuable because the people see the physicians working out in the community, not necessarily doing health-care things, and this builds trust. Actually, one of the things we tell our residents is they cannot provide health-care services when working with community partners. Now, these communities could use health-care services, but we wanted them to think about health in the broader sense. We did not want the residents to go out there and see patients and give shots, because it is easy to fall into your old line of thinking. What else can we do to change that social environment, change that environment to try to improve health?

One of our residents has done a radio show in Russian to the Russian community, where she answered questions about health. Another one did a newsletter. Someone did an art mural about exercise. Another took a group of very disadvantaged kids on a trip to Yosemite and opened their eyes to nature; kids who had never left their neighborhood and did not even realize that Yosemite existed. Another one worked with teens who were failing school, talked about life opportunities, and really tried to empower people about their health by thinking positively about their future.

The principles we use in CPT are around asset-based community development. Medicine teaches doctors to ask people why they are here, what is your problem. We always want to find and solve that problem. However, we teach our residents to actually look at people's assets—not just to look at people and neighborhoods as being problems, but to look at them as being assets. They have assets to contribute. We consider asset-based community development as sort of the basic science of our outreach program. We teach the residents how to form effective partnerships with communities. I think if we can get health-care people to connect with communities and form these partnerships and teach community partners how to effectively partner with health care, we can think about new and creative ways to try to improve health.

An example of a health-care intervention is the High/Scope Perry Preschool Project.[17] This is a randomized, controlled study where they had two groups of kids that they have been following for forty years now. All are from similar neighborhoods but one group went to preschool and the other did not. Arrest rates are more than five times by age forty for the no-program group, while the program group has a much lower rate of arrests. In California we spend $23,000 a year per prisoner; that is like a college education for every year we keep someone in prison. The people who were in the preschool program were also much more likely to have a higher income. When we think about how to improve health, we have to think about things we can do in education, for example, not just about health care.

Health care itself is a sector and an engine of economic growth. We do not want to just willy-nilly expand the health-care sector; we do know there is a demand for that and that also could be an employment engine as well. Just in the greater Sacramento region, there is growth for jobs in health care[18] and with our aging population that will continue to be an opportunity for employment growth. It would be nice if we could invest more in prevention and spend some of that to hire people who concentrate on prevention, and not lay off our public health nurses in the county.

> "Smart growth and decisions around land use are...very important because they have impacts on health."

Smart growth and decisions around land use are going to be very important because they have impacts on health. People need access to land for recreation, not just for fun's sake, but for health's sake. Transportation is important—not just how to get to health-care facilities, but how to get to work, how to get to your shopping, how to create less air pollution, which leads to emphysema, lung cancer, and asthma.

The California Health Interview Survey (CHIS) is a wonderful resource for California. However, unless you are looking for data from a large urban area, the data is not very useful, because we do not have sufficient data for many rural communities. We really need to push forward so that we have sufficient data to measure what is happening in our rural communities, what is happening in the Central Valley. We need to collect more data so we know where we are going.

The National Children's Study is going to be the largest study of children in the country. They are going to follow one hundred thousand children while looking at environmental influences on their health. Sacramento County is one of the study sites for this. It is important to do these studies and look at exactly what the influence of these factors is and therefore understand what the most effective thing is that we can do to improve the health of our communities.

Prevention is extremely important to insure that we all have a healthier future. We have many ways of ameliorating disease and helping people, but it's better not to let it happen in the first place. Prevention can lead to longer health, may lead to lower cost, certainly lower health-care costs in the future. Prevention itself, though, does cost money and so it is an upfront investment in having a healthier future. It is more important to make that up-front investment and stay healthy than try to cure or treat someone later on.

I am a big believer in the concept of social capital. We need to figure out how to connect people together, because many of us are operating in different silos; most of my health-care colleagues are not thinking about land use and water and all these other topics. How do we break down the barriers between the different silos and realize these are all interconnected? That is part of the discussion about where we want to be and where we want to go. We need to help people realize that their interest is not just about that one narrow issue; there are other interests they may also have that they care about that are tied into this at multiple different levels. It is not just going to be at the top with President Obama declaring this for the federal government, it is not just going to be the state government deciding, it is going to be people and communities coming together. One of the things we learned in our CPT program is that there is power in just getting people connected and working together and redefining the social norms in those communities. It is not just going to be decision makers and policy makers, it is also going to be about people coming together in their communities, saying, "This is what we want for our community," and then working together to move that forward. There is an opportunity for us here in the Valley, if we could figure out how it all works together, from south of Bakersfield to north of Redding: despite all the diversity we have in the Great Valley, we can come together to have that kind of conversation through organizations like the Great Valley Center, to talk about what kind of future we want and how all these pieces interconnect.

In terms of what is going to happen in 2020 in the Central Valley, I would say again, I do not know any more than any of you. I think it depends on what we are all collectively willing to do. Are we willing to make those investments in prevention? Are we willing to make those investments in education? Are we willing to make the land use decisions? It will depend upon what we are willing to do, our political will, and our determination to make it a better 2020 than just following the trend line.

Valley-Wise Living

Things you can do between now and 2020 for a sustainable Valley

1. Establish a medical home—a physician or care provider you see regularly—and let them get to know you.

2. Demand that culturally literate prevention and health education resources are available in your community.

3. Do something to improve the environment.

4. Pick one issue and join a grassroots coalition or organization working on that issue.

5. Do the simple things you can do to improve your health first.

6. Park in the back of parking lots and walk in.

7. Schedule a get-together with a friend while walking around a track instead of meeting for coffee.

8. Quit smoking.

9. Do not underestimate the importance of personal mental health. Gauge your stress levels and practice strategies to reduce your stress. If your company has a wellness program, join it.

10. Enroll your small one in a preschool program.

Resources

Recommended Reports and Books

The Spirit Catches You and You Fall Down: A Hmong Child, Her American Doctors, and the Collision of Two Cultures
Anne Fadiman
New York: Farrar, Straus and Giroux, 1997

"How to Create and Implement Healthy General Plans"
Public Health Law and Policy/Planning for Healthy Places
Free download available at: www.healthyplanning.org/toolkit_healthygp.html

"Measuring the Health Effects of Sprawl"
Smart Growth America
Free download available at www.smartgrowthamerica.org/health.html

More on the Web

Health-related

Central Valley Health Policy Institute, California State University, Fresno: www.csufresno.edu/ccchhs/institutes_programs/CVHPI/index.shtml

California Department of Public Health: www.cdph.ca.gov

Network for a Healthy California: www.networkforahealthycalifornia.net

Winters Healthcare Foundation: www.wintershealth.org

National Children's Study: www.nationalchildrensstudy.gov

California Health Interview Survey: www.chis.ucla.edu

Communities and Physicians Together: www.cpt-online.org

California Children's Health Initiatives: www.cchi4kids.org
(Sacramento region: www.coverthekids.com)

California HealthCare Foundation: www.chcf.org

Education-related

Preschool California: www.preschoolcalifornia.org

Reading and Beyond: www.readingandbeyond.org

California Reading and Literature Project:
http://csmp.ucop.edu/projects/view/crlp

California Afterschool Network: www.afterschoolnetwork.org

Youth In Focus: www.youthinfocus.net

Californians Together: www.californianstogether.org

Institute of Higher Education Leadership and Policy, Sacramento State
University: www.csus.edu/ihelp

Food for Thought

Questions for more discussion

1.   What are the three most important social determinants of illness in our community?

2.   What resources do I (or my organization) need in order to address priority social determinants of illness? Who can be invited to join the effort?

3.   How will our community look different if these social determinants of illness are addressed? What can be done in one year? five years? ten years?[19]

About the Great Valley Center

The Great Valley Center (GVC) is a unique organization whose mission is to improve the economic, social, and environmental well-being of California's Great Central Valley. A non-advocacy, nonpartisan organization, GVC was founded in 1997 as a nonprofit 501(c)(3) to provide resources and support as the region deals with tremendous issues of growth and change. It is the only nongovernmental organization that focuses on the Central Valley region, a vast nineteen-county area stretching more than 450 miles, from Redding to Bakersfield. Through both core programs and partnerships with other organizations, GVC encourages dialogue among the Valley's many interests, supports collaborative local efforts, and ensures broad community access to the most up-to-date economic, environmental, and social data regarding the Great Central Valley. GVC is headquartered in Modesto, with satellite offices in Chico and Bakersfield.

The initial funders of the Great Valley Center—the William and Flora Hewlett Foundation, the James Irvine Foundation, and the David and Lucile Packard Foundation—supported the creation of GVC as a regional intermediary with a broad mandate to engage in a number of strategies that would increase the long-term sustainability of the Central Valley.

The Great Valley Center formed a partnership with the University of California, Merced, in 2005 to ensure the institutional sustainability of the organization and leverage the resources of a research university with the community connections of the Great Valley Center. GVC continues to operate with an independent board of directors and raises all its operating revenue.

The Great Valley Center is giving a new pride and recognition to a region that has long been unrecognized and underestimated for its contributions to the state and nation. GVC continues to work on a regionwide basis to improve the Valley's chances for a more successful future as it strives to achieve parity with the rest of the state and nation. GVC works on behalf of all residents to improve the Valley's quality of life, to call attention to its many rich traditions and extraordinary assets, and to ensure our future is one in which we can all take pride. GVC's publications, promotions, and events call statewide and even national attention to the rich traditions and varied assets of the Central Valley.

A one-of-a-kind resource, the Great Valley Center gathers people from all walks of life representing an extraordinary array of interests to talk, listen, and plan together. GVC is trusted by community leaders, business leaders, farmers, teachers, elected officials, policy makers, and many others to facilitate planning for the Valley's future. The GVC's neutrality and expert leadership overcome barriers between people and interests, ensuring that different visions are heard and the most workable ideas are advanced. With leadership programs, new strategies for economic development, and a vision for a Valley that successfully balances economic, social, and environmental needs, GVC staff is working every day to bring people together to solve the area's most difficult challenges.

Lessons Learned (so far)

Policy makers follow the public more than they lead.
In order to facilitate real change, there has to be a population that believes in those desired outcomes. Apathy and acceptance of underperformance is common. In many Central Valley communities, and indeed the region at large, the unity has to be built, along with aspiration, vision, and a sense of the possible. Part of the strategy for the region is to teach people how to think about problems differently and ask better questions.

Work with people and communities where they are.
There is no value in expending resources on projects that are neither internally motivated nor locally supported, no matter how worthy the goal. In the Valley, there are many communities that either through a limited vision or because of limited capacity are not ready to make significant changes or long-term commitments. Limited resources are best focused where there is local interest and commitment to problem solving.

People can be motivated by ideas and information.

Many cities, counties, and community-based organizations in the region have had little experience with strategies and devices employed effectively outside the region for social action, community development, successful partnering, or collaboration. Providing access to new ideas and technical support to implement them can be hugely valuable, and in many cases can provide opportunities for improved implementation and positive change. Almost every discussion in the community begins with the priority for more jobs, before the environment, housing costs, education, health care, or community development. Developing a more sophisticated and strategic plan for economic development takes experience and somewhat savvy leadership.

Racial, cultural, and linguistic segregation are unspoken but significant barriers.

Effective community action and representative governance cannot happen without valuing and incorporating diversity. Local elections are still dominated by an "old guard" in most communities, in spite of changing demographics. Leadership development in underrepresented populations is essential to enable a successful transition to more representative leadership. Community development and social capital concerns are still best addressed at the community level, though there are demonstrated benefits in establishing networks that cross local boundaries so that people can learn from and be supported by others in the region who are dealing with the same or similar problems.

Each community has assets that can be supported.

From its inception, GVC aimed to support the good things that people were trying to accomplish, and in so doing foster progress and sustainability without having to be judgmental or critical of local priorities. Work can be done locally or sub-regionally while promoting a regional context. This continues to be an indispensable strategy.

Past Accomplishments

Here are just a few examples of programs that have been completed:

The Great Valley Center's **LEGACI** grant program provided seed money for new activities and re-granted almost $5 million of foundation funds over six years to support and encourage a variety of groups and activities that would move the region toward more progressive thinking and more inclusive practices. LEGACI is an acronym representing a focus on Land use, Economic development, Growth, Agriculture, and Community Investment. The grants were used to provide resources for community planning, economic development activities, support the arts and cultural awareness, encourage resource conservation, assist culturally diverse groups in starting businesses, learn about farming, and engage with community leadership.

The **Agricultural Transaction Program** (ATP) provided Valley communities with resources to permanently conserve significant agricultural lands, influence growth patterns, promote public policies and programs supportive of conservation in the region, act as a catalyst for local efforts, strengthen capacity of groups working to conserve agricultural land, and leverage resources with other sources of funding. At the close of the program ATP invested $4.5 million dollars in transactional funding in three Valley communities which funded twenty conservation easements, protecting over twenty-one thousand acres of Valley farmland, and attracted more than $35,000,000 in matching funds.

For three years the Great Valley Center's **Highway 99 Task Force** brought together stakeholders from the San Joaquin Valley to plan for growth and enhancement along California's "Main Street." In 2007 that culminated with a state bond of $1 billion allocated for improvements to the corridor.

The California Department of Transportation (Caltrans) and the Great Valley Center, with the support of the American Institute of Architects' California Council and private organizations, partnered in an open one-stage international competition to select a design and design team for a self-sustainable and "off the grid" roadside *GreenStop*—the word coined to designate a **green roadside rest area**. As a transitional outcome of this project, two rest stops along Highway 99—Tipton and Turlock—now have wireless Internet available free to travelers.

The **Central Valley Digital Network** worked in conjunction with Ameri-Corps VISTA to narrow the digital divide. To reduce the disparity between the technological haves and have-nots, this program operated at twenty-five community-based sites in ten counties and provided more than forty-one thousand individual user sessions, facilitated the establishment of Community Technology Centers, and put the first Spanish-language computers into the San Joaquin Valley.

Almost six hundred individuals and organizations were able to take advantage of training, coaching, and/or organizational development activities offered through CAPs, the **Community-based Assistance Program** that brought professional assistance to nonprofits throughout the region. The organizations that participated in those programs reported more than $12 million in new funding in the first year after the program was completed.

Four community foundations, working with the Great Valley Center and the Youth Leadership Institute, established local **Grants Advisory Boards for Youth** (GABY), youth-to-youth granting programs through each of the four community foundations in Shasta, Sacramento, Fresno, and Kern Counties. They committed to continue the programs with their own resources for at least three years.

The **Scenarios Project** offered alternative views of the future in each of the three main sub-regions of the Valley, inspired a citizen-led land use initiative, framed the discussion about the future of education in dozens of school districts, provided the background and context for general plan processes in several communities, and motivated non-English-speaking youth to become more engaged in their communities. The programs have been incorporated into high school and college curricula and are used to demonstrate why engagement and participation matter at every level.

The Great Valley Center's **Citi Success Fund**, in partnership with Citi Foundation, was a granting program that equipped teachers with essential funding for educating through innovative means. Projects included support for an elementary school in Fresno with a listening center so that struggling readers, English learners, and special education students could participate more fully in their classrooms, and support for a project inspiring high school students in Galt to create original poetry by commercially recording it for a podcast.

CATAPULT leadership training empowered high-potential teenagers to realize their potential to become leaders in the region. CATAPULT participants have gone on to attend colleges and universities throughout the Valley and nation.

These programs have been successful in a variety of venues and have created networks that have contributed to better public policy outcomes, and they have supported an increase in the diversity and representation of community-level leadership.

Current Focus

Increasingly reliant on multiple funders and sponsors, GVC has been aggressively engaged in new focus for its work that will contribute to its mission of increasing the capacity of the region to act better on its own behalf. The Great Valley Center is currently focused in these three areas:

1. Data, Information, and Resources

The Great Valley Center, through its "Assessing the Region via Indicators" report series, project reports, white papers, and publications, has become a trusted and credible provider of information about the region. This information is available free to be used by anyone, anywhere in the world. Many of the GVC reports and recommendations recognize the smaller "regions within the region"—the Sacramento River Valley in the north, the Sacramento metropolitan region, and the San Joaquin Valley in the south—in separate data sets or distinct publications. This organizational component—data, information, and resources—includes indicator reports, the GVC website, information and referrals, public education and outreach, conferences, and seminars and convenings, all designed to provide knowledge and information to and about the region. GVC-sponsored studies, conferences, and publications provide much-needed information on the status of life in the Valley, as well as updates in laws and policies, to help nonprofits, businesses, and elected officials better meet the needs of residents. Each year the Great Valley Center hosts an annual conference, as well as the Sacramento Valley Forum in the northern part of the state. From agritourism to dealing with growth and regional planning, the Great Valley Center is focusing on the issues and opportunities in all parts of our Valley. Additionally, with its affiliation with the University of California, Merced, GVC is growing its research focus as the university adds students and faculty.

2. Leadership Development

Through the Institute for the Development of Emerging Area Leaders (IDEAL), the Great Valley Leadership Institute (GVLI), and the Great Valley chapter of the American Leadership Forum (ALF), GVC continues to offer high-quality regional leadership training opportunities for emerging community leaders, elected officials, and experienced leaders. In these nationally recognized leadership institutes, more than two hundred emerging leaders have completed the IDEAL curriculum focused on real issues and service projects to train those who are the region's future. Elected officials in GVLI are trained by faculty members of Harvard University, Massachusetts Institute of Technology, and Columbia University to better represent their constituents and shape policy by spending more than four days focusing on ethics, problem solving, and representative decision making. Beginning in 2009, a new chapter of ALF was formed for more experienced leaders to be better able to address challenges for the region, their workplace, and personal life. Facilitated by nationally known experts, ALF class members establish relationships that build trust and cooperation and are armed with new skills for taking on difficult issues, appreciating diverse views, and identifying resources to turn dialogue into action.

3. Regional Projects

As the area develops a greater sense of region, there is more work to be done to remove the barriers between people, ideas, and plans. The Great Valley Center's regional programs are building a foundation for a better quality of life in the Valley. GVC provides staff support for aspects of the San Joaquin Valley Blueprint Planning Process, which developed a blueprint for all eight counties. A blueprint provides a context for land use and transportation decisions made at the local level. GVC also provides support to the California Partnership for the San Joaquin Valley, particularly the Land Use, Housing and Agriculture, Advanced Communications Systems, and Energy work groups. These projects require coordination, communication, consensus building, and convening, all established competencies of GVC.

The Pixley Connect program bridges the divide between the information superhighway and the region's poor communities. GVC delivers computers into the hands and homes of youth in poor communities and trains them, not only to use the computers, but also to program and repair them. In its Agricultural and Land Trust programs, GVC helps farmers preserve their way of life and conserve their land. Agriculture and Land Trust programs keep farmers on their land, protecting the food supply, conserving open space, and ensuring that agriculture remains an economic driver for the Valley. The GVC's Energy Program works on several levels, from helping cities audit their energy use and develop local responses to global warming to distributing energy efficient lightbulbs to residents of the

Valley. Additionally, GVC helps communities grow urban forests and incorporate green standards into municipal codes.

There are still plenty of challenges for the Great Valley as the region moves toward a more sustainable future. We hope that by reading this book you have become excited to learn about our collective future and take positive actions, even in the face of cynicism and chronic problems. We will thrive, not just survive.

Programs of the Great Valley Center are made possible through the support of individuals, companies, and philanthropic foundations working to support the region as its communities plan for the future. GVC relies on a core of dedicated volunteers and frequently partners with other organizations and government agencies to efficiently address important issues affecting the region.

If you would like to make a contribution, please visit us online at www. greatvalley.org or mail to:

Great Valley Center
201 Needham Street
Modesto, California 95354

The Great Valley Center is a nonprofit organization under section 501(c)(3) of the IRS code. Federal ID #77-0450770. All contributions to the Great Valley Center are tax deductible.

Notes

L. Hunter Lovins, "The Sustainability Imperative"

1. California's state unemployment rate hit 11.5 percent in May 2009, ranking fifth highest. Among the 372 metropolitan statistical areas in the U.S., Central Valley areas have some of the highest unemployment rates: Merced (3rd highest, 18.3%); Yuba City (4th, 18.2%); Modesto (6th, 16.8%); Stockton (7th, 15.6%); Fresno (9th, 15.5%); Visalia-Porterville (10th, 15.4%); Redding (11th, 15.4%); Hanford-Corcoran (12th, 15.3%); Madera-Chowchilla (16th, 14.6%); and Chico (34th, 12.4%). Source: U.S. Department of Labor, Bureau of Labor Statistics, "Unemployment Rates for Metropolitan Areas, Not Seasonally Adjusted, April 2009," last modified June 3, 2009.

2. Lester R. Brown is an influential environmentalist. He served as founder for the Worldwatch Institute and is currently the president of the Earth Policy Institute, which are both environmental research organizations.

3. Steven Chu, PhD, was appointed Secretary of Energy for the United States government under the Obama administration. He was awarded the Nobel Prize in the discipline of physics in 1997. He has directed the prestigious Lawrence Berkeley National Laboratory and has served as a professor at Stanford University. He is a major proponent of alternative energy systems to help suspend the decline in Earth's environmental future.

4. James E. Hansen, PhD, is a National Aeronautics and Space Administration (NASA) researcher. He is a physicist, astronomer, and mathematician. He has devoted most of his efforts to understanding climates, however. He performs climatology research at the NASA Goddard Institute for Space Studies and advocates curtailing adverse impacts on Earth's climate caused by harmful environmental byproducts. He is currently researching the effects of radioactive transfer on climate.

5. Holmes Hummel received his PhD from Stanford University in environment and resources. He is now a congressional science fellow helping facilitate the exchange of prominent scientific climate research and political policy. He works in concord with Congressman Jay Inslee and looks forward to a professorship at the University of California, Berkeley.

6. Bill Becker currently holds the Wirth Chair in Environmental and Community Development Policy at the University of Colorado, Denver. He is a community and environmental champion. He formerly directed the United States Department of Energy's Central Regional Office. There he helped implement developments in alternative energies and the advancement of energy efficiency, especially in how to impact communities. Becker began his career in alternative energy development when he helped author and carry out a project which helped a flooded Wisconsin area move locations and start a solar community.

7. Ray Anderson is currently an environmental entrepreneur. He founded and acts as chairman of the company Interface Inc. and has made major advancements in environmental business ethnics. His company is a global supplier of carpet fabrics. Since 1995 he has helped improve the company's waste production and he continues to work on making his business more sustainable.

8. Andrew Winston received his BA in economics from Princeton, an MBA from Columbia, and a master's in economics from Yale. He is the coauthor of *Green to Gold: How Smart Companies Use Environmental Strategy to Innovate, Create Value, and Build Competitive Advantage* (Westchester Book Services, 2006). In it, he promotes the establishment of companies that use environmentally sound and sustainable practices to advantage in business.

9. Pasquale Pistorio is the board chairman for STMicroelectronics, and the former president and CEO. He has worked diligently to expand the company's sustainable practices. He subscribes to the belief that companies such as STMicroelectronics should encourage the advancement of the environmental movement. Pistorio believes that modern companies should complete more than the moral minimum, pursuing higher ethics and social consciousness, and that if companies like STMicroelectronics continue to do valuable work in the promotion of sustainability, it will influence the next generation of employees and other companies to do the same.

10. The California Lighting Technology Center (CLTC), based at the University of California at Davis, opened in 2003 to improve and advance the distribution of energy efficiency by providing research in lighting technology. The center educates the community about the benefits of energy-efficient lighting practices and then

advises on implementation. CLTC partners with various vendors to help pursue its mission. Website: www.cltc.ucdavis.edu.

11. Natural Capitalism Solutions is a company that provides a number of green services. Website: www.natcapsolutions.com.

12. Fisk, "Health and Productivity Gains from Better Indoor Environments," in "The Role of Emerging Energy-Efficient Technology in Promoting Workplace Productivity and Health" (Lawrence Berkeley National Laboratory, February 2002).

13. Matthew R. Simmons, *Twilight in the Desert: The Coming Saudi Oil Shock and the World Economy* (Hoboken, NJ: John Wiley & Sons, Inc, 2005).

14. The two most noted contributions of M. King Hubbert to the field of geology are the Hubbert curve and Hubbert peak theory. Hubbert's advances in the study of geology caused the government to make some crucial policy changes.

15. Robert James Woolsey Jr. is an expert in foreign policy and served as the director of the U.S. Central Intelligence Agency during the Bush Administration.

16. The English entrepreneur Sir Richard Charles Nicholas Branson started the highly successful Virgin Group, which consists of a multitude of businesses and includes a major record label and an airline.

17. City Information Services Limited (CityIS Ltd., www.cityis.com), is a worldwide visual communication company.

18. Van Jones founded and is the president of Green For All and served as the Special Advisor for Green Jobs and Enterprises under the Obama administration. He is a humanitarian, human rights activist, environmentalist, attorney, and published author.

19. Thomas Jefferson to George Washington, 1787, in Bergh and Lipscomb, eds., *The Writings of Thomas Jefferson,* Memorial Edition (Thomas Jefferson Memorial Association, 1903), 6:277.

20. Bob Willard, a noteworthy name in sustainable business practices, worked for over three decades for IBM in a variety of positions.

21. Goldman Sachs Investment Research, GS SUSTAIN List, which includes companies that have been selected by their environmental, social, and government (ESG) framework, 2007.

22. Richard Florida, PhD, specializes in urban and economic matters. He is a professor at the University of Toronto and the leader of a consulting firm.

23. A. T. Kearney, "'Green' Winners: The Performance of Sustainability-focused Companies during the Financial Crisis" (A. T. Kearney, November 2008).

24. A special assessment is a funding mechanism for infrastructure projects that appears on property tax bills. Solar assessment districts are slightly different in that property owners volunteer to participate in the program and the amount they are taxed depends on the amount of money they borrow and the loan term.

25. Adam Smith (1723–1790) was a pioneer of modern economics and the author of many books that expressed his ideologies and philosophies.

26. LASER: Local Action for Sustainable Economic Renewal, Guide to Community Development can be downloaded for free at: www.natcapsolutions.org/projects/LASER/LASERguide.pdf. This is a tool kit for citizens within a community to build a sustainable, locally based economy and do it themselves.

Quentin Kopp, "Designing the Transportation of the Future"

1. American Society of Civil Engineers California, Infrastructure Report Card, www.ascecareportcard.org.

2. "California's High Speed Rail," Center for Regional Change, UC Davis, http://regionalchange.ucdavisdu/resources/about-regional-change/ californias-high-speed-rail

3. ASCE California, Infrastructure Report Card.

A. G. Kawamura, "A Thriving Agriculture in the Twenty-First Century

1. Carol Whiteside, Ag Aware Luncheon speech, Modesto, California, April 7, 2005.

2. California Department of Water Resources publications can be accessed at www.water.ca.gov.

3. Draper, Robert, "Australia's Dry Run." *National Geographic*, April 2009.

4. More information about California's Agriculture Vision 2030 is available from the California Department of Food and Agriculture at www.cdfa.ca.gov/agvision.

Jeff Mount, "The Delta's Age of Reason"

1. Lund, Jay, Ellen Hanak, William Fleenor, Richard Howitt, Jeffrey Mount, and Peter Moyle. *Envisioning Futures for the Sacramento–San Joaquin Delta* (Public Policy Institute of California, 2007).

2. UC Davis, Center for Watershed Sciences.

3. Ibid.

4. Zito, Kelly. "Peripheral Canal Urged to Save the Delta." *San Francisco Chronicle,* July 18, 2008.

5. Mount, Jeff, and Jay Lund. "The Delta: Managing the Inevitable." *Contra Costa Times,* May 2, 2009.

6. In 2004 a U.S. Fish and Wildlife Service (FWS) biological assessment determined that the existing Operations, Criteria, and Plan (OCAP) did not jeopardize the continued existence of the delta smelt or its critical habitat. That opinion was invalidated in May 2007 by Judge Oliver Wanger. In August 2007, Wanger ruled to protect the delta smelt by curtailing water deliveries through the State Water Project (SWP) and Central Valley Project (CVP). The ruling has highlighted the potential long-term economic effects of water shortage due to problems with Delta conveyance, diminishing water supplies, and lack of adequate storage.

Richard Pan, "A Community Approach to Health and Health Care"

1. California Department of Education, DataQuest, Standards and Assessment Division, http://dq.cde.ca.gov/dataquest, last accessed April 29, 2009.

2. KVIE Public Television and Great Valley Center, *2020 Foresight: The Valley in 10 Years,* taped April 2009. Fred Myer was interviewed by David Hosley. ©2009, Great Valley Center.

3. KVPT Public Television and Great Valley Center, *What's Killing People in the Central Valley,* taped June 2009. Sophia Pagoulatos was interviewed by David Hosley. ©2009, Great Valley Center.

4. U.S. Department of Commerce, Bureau of the Census.

5. CDC/NCHS, National Vital Statistics System, Mortality.

6. Centers for Medicare and Medicaid Services, Office of the Actuary, National Health Statistics Group.

7. Kaiser/HRET Survey of Employer-Sponsored Health Benefits.

8. Evans, R. G., M. L. Barer, and T. R. Marmor, eds. *Why Are Some People Healthy and Others Not? The Determinants of Health of Populations* (New York: Aldine de Gruyter, 1994).

9. Schroder, S. A. "We Can Do Better—Improving the Health of the American People." *New England Journal of Medicine* 357:12, 1221–1228.

10. Kuh, Diana, and Yoav Ben-Shlomo. "A Life Course Approach to Chronic Disease Epidemiology: Conceptual Models, Empirical Challenges and Interdisciplinary Perspectives." *International Journal of Epidemiology* 31:2, 285–293.

11. Chenowith, David. "The Economic Costs of Physical Inactivity, Obesity, and Overweight in California Adults: Health Care, Workers' Compensation, and Lost Productivity." California Department of Health Services, April 2005.

12. Koplan, J. P., C. T. Liverman, and V. A. Kraak, eds. *Preventing Childhood Obesity: Health in the Balance* (Washington, DC: National Academies Press, 2005).

13. Gordon-Larsen, P., M. C. Nelson, P. Page, B. M. Popkin. "Inequality in the Built Environment Underlies Key Health Disparities in Physical Activity and Obesity." *Pediatrics* 117:2, 417–424.

14. Great Valley Center, "The State of the Great Central Valley of California: Assessing the Region via Indicators—Public Health and Access to Care," 2d ed. (Modesto, CA: Great Valley Center, 2008). Available free at www.greatvalley.org.

15. Starfield, Barbara, and Leiyu Shi. "The Medical Home, Access to Care, and Insurance: a Review of Evidence." *Pediatrics* 113:5, 1493–1498.

16. Anderson, L. M., S. C. Scrimshaw, M. T. Fullilove, and J. E. Fielding, and the Task Force on Community Preventive Services. "The *Community Guide's* Model for Linking the Social Environment to Health. *American Journal of Preventive Medicine* 24:Suppl 3, 12–20.

17. Schweinhart L. J. *The High/Scope Perry Preschool Study through Age 40.* Ypsilanti, MI: HighScope Press, 2005.

18. Center for the Continuing Study of the California Economy.

19. Brennan Ramirez, L. K., E. Baker, M. Metzler. *Promoting Health Equity: A Resource to Help Communities Address Social Determinants of Health* (Atlanta: U.S. Department of Health and Human Services, Centers for Disease Control and Prevention, 2008). This publication is available at http://www.cdc.gov/nccdphp/dach/chaps and http://www.transtria.com/resources.php.

HEYDAY INSTITUTE

Since its founding in 1974, Heyday Books has occupied a unique niche in the publishing world, specializing in books that foster an understanding of the history, literature, art, environment, social issues, and culture of California and the West. We are a 501(c)(3) nonprofit organization based in Berkeley, California, serving a wide range of people and audiences.

We are grateful for the generous funding we've received for our publications and programs during the past year from foundations and more than three hundred and fifty individual donors. Major supporters include:

Anonymous; Audubon California; Judith and Phillip Auth; Barona Band of Mission Indians; B.C.W. Trust III; S. D. Bechtel, Jr. Foundation; Barbara and Fred Berensmeier; Berkeley Civic Arts Program and Civic Arts Commission; Joan Berman; Peter and Mimi Buckley; Lewis and Sheana Butler; Butler Koshland Fund; California State Automobile Association; California State Coastal Conservancy; California State Library; Joanne Campbell; Candelaria Fund; John and Nancy Cassidy Family Foundation, through Silicon Valley Community Foundation; Creative Work Fund; Columbia Foundation; The Community Action Fund; Community Futures Collective; Compton Foundation, Inc.; Lawrence Crooks; Ida Rae Egli; Donald and Janice Elliott, in honor of David Elliott, through Silicon Valley Community Foundation; Evergreen Foundation; Federated Indians of Graton Rancheria; Mark and Tracy Ferron; Furthur Foundation; George Gamble; Wallace Alexander Gerbode Foundation; Richard & Rhoda Goldman Fund; Ben Graber, in honor of Sandy Graber; Evelyn & Walter Haas, Jr. Fund; Walter & Elise Haas Fund; James and Coke Hallowell; Cheryl Hinton; James Irvine Foundation; Marty and Pamela Krasney; Robert and Karen Kustel, in honor of Bruce Kelley; Guy Lampard and Suzanne Badenhoop; LEF Foundation; Michael McCone; National Endowment for the Arts; National Park Service; Organize Training Center; Patagonia; Pease Family Fund, in honor of Bruce Kelley; Resources Legacy Fund; Alan Rosenus; San Francisco Foundation; San Manuel Band of Mission Indians; Deborah Sanchez; Contee and Maggie Seely; James B. Swinerton; Swinerton Family Fund; Taproot Foundation; Thendara Foundation; Lisa Van Cleef and Mark Gunson; Marion Weber; Albert and Susan Wells; Dean Witter Foundation; and Yocha Dehe Wintun Nation.

For more information about Heyday Institute, our publications and programs, please visit our website at www.heydaybooks.com.

green press
INITIATIVE

Heyday Books is committed to preserving ancient forests and natural resources. We elected to print this title on 100% post consumer recycled paper, processed chlorine free. As a result, for this printing, we have saved:

21 Trees (40' tall and 6-8" diameter)
7 Million BTUs of Total Energy
1,976 Pounds of Greenhouse Gases
9,519 Gallons of Wastewater
578 Pounds of Solid Waste

Heyday Books made this paper choice because our printer, Thomson-Shore, Inc., is a member of Green Press Initiative, a nonprofit program dedicated to supporting authors, publishers, and suppliers in their efforts to reduce their use of fiber obtained from endangered forests.

For more information, visit www.greenpressinitiative.org

Environmental impact estimates were made using the Environmental Defense Paper Calculator. For more information visit: www.papercalculator.org.